Language Crimes

THE LANGUAGE LIBRARY

EDITED BY DAVID CRYSTAL

Language Crimes

The Use and Abuse of Language Evidence in the Courtroom

Roger W. Shuy

First published 1993
First published in paperback 1996
Reprinted 1997

Blackwell Publishers Inc
350 Main Street
Malden, Massachusetts 02148, USA

Blackwell Publishers Ltd
108 Cowley Road
Oxford OX4 1JF, UK

Library of Congress Cataloging in Publication Data
Shuy, Roger W.
Language crimes: the use and abuse of language evidence in the
courtroom / Roger W. Shuy
p.   cm. — (The Language Library)
Includes bibliographical references (p.   ) and index.
ISBN 0–631–18618–2 (hb) — ISBN 0–631–20153–X (pb)
1. Forensic linguistics–United States. 2. Evidence, Criminal–United States–
Language. 3. Audiotapes in courtroom proceedings–United
States. 3. Linguistic analysis (Linguistics) I. Title. II. Series
KF8968.54.S48   1993
345.73'064—dc20
[347.30564]   92–17369   CIP

British Library Cataloguing in Publication Data
A CIP catalogue record for this book is available from the British Library

Typeset in 11 on 12.5pt Sabon
by Graphicraft Typesetters Limited, Hong Kong
Printed and bound in Great Britain
by Athenæum Press Ltd, Gateshead, Tyne & Wear

This book is printed on acid-free paper

Contents

Foreword

Dr Roger Shuy's *Language Crimes* is an important book. Through the use of materials taken from a series of actual criminal prosecutions, Shuy amply shows the value of sophisticated linguistic analysis for the proper interpretation of oral conversations recorded on electronic tape. Shuy's book, too, is easily read by those without a technical background in linguistics, as he keeps his use of professional jargon to the minimum. As such, *Language Crimes* should be read – and studied – by all those involved in investigating, prosecuting, defending, and judging in the administration of justice.

The interpretation of language is an old concern of the legal profession. Usually, that language is written, and it is in the form of statutes, judicial decision, or legal instruments (e.g., contracts, deeds, or wills). Indeed, the first systematic discussion of statutory interpretation in Anglo-American jurisprudence was penned anonymously around 1567. (Frankfurter, "Some Reflections on the Reading of Statutes," 47, *Column L. Rev.* 527, 544 (1947)) The common law subsequently codified its canons of construction well before the American Revolution in a series of Latin maxims that are still cited by the courts, though their use reached its acme during the ascendancy of the scientific jurisprudence of the nineteenth century, when they were thought to operate in the formal fashion of logic. Today, the maxims are recognized as little more than "axioms of experience." (*Boston Sand & Gravel Co. v. United States*, 278 US 41, 48 (1928) (Holmes, J.)). They are, in Searle's apt phraseology, "regulative" rather than "constitutive." (J. R. Searle, *Speech Acts: An Essay in the Philosophy of Language* 33 (1969)). It must be candidly conceded, therefore, that the maxims are not always determinative of outcome (compare

Herman & MacLean v. Huddleston, 459 US 375, 387 n.23 (1983) (rejecting *expressio unius est exclusio alterius* in an interpretation of the Securities and Exchange Act of 1934) with *Passenger Corp. v. passenger Ass'n*, 414 US 453, 458 (1974) (accepting *expressio* etc. in a construction of the Rail Passenger Service Act of 1970)), and they sometimes, in fact, point in opposite directions (compare *The Pedro*, 175 US 354, 364 (1899) (*verbis plane expressis omnino standum est*) with *Green v. Liter and Others*, 12 US 229, 248 (1844) (*cessante ratione legis, cessat et ipsa lex*)). Nevertheless, the point remains that the legal profession is steeped in the process of interpretation. That is not to say that fierce arguments do not occur in the profession over the political as well as linguistic propriety of various theories of interpretation. They do. (See, for example, *Interpreting the Constitution: The Debate over Original Intent* (1990, J. Rakove ed.)) The point is not that agreement is universal, but that the terms of such debates are the stuff of everyday professional experience for lawyers – advocates as well as judges.

Unfortunately, the profession is without a similar history of experience in the interpretation of recorded oral conversation. We are now only at the beginning of that development. Indeed, the microphone, telephone, and dictograph were not invented until the last half of the nineteenth century. Accordingly, the use of the product of these inventions in the administration of justice is primarily a phenomenon of the twentieth century. The first reported appellate opinion upholding the introduction in evidence of a phonograph did not come until 1906. (*Boyne City, G. & A. R. Co. v. Anderson*, 146 Mich. 328, 109 NW 429 (1906)). The next appellate opinion did not come for 24 years. (*Com'm v. Roller*, 100 Pa. Super Ct. 125 (1930) (upholding the introduction of a sound motion picture of a confession)). The first use of a surreptitious recording noted in an appellate opinion followed six years later. (*Com'm v. Clark*, 123 Pa. Supr. Ct. 277, 187 A. 237 (1936) (upholding the introduction of a speak-o-phone disk recording of a bribery attempt of the attorney general)). Shuy's experience as a linguist interpreting recorded oral conversations in court, therefore, is on the frontier of theory and practice of the law in this area.

In 1966, I was a consultant on the legal aspects of the investigation of organized crime to the President's Crime Commission, which recommended the adoption of comprehensive legislation regulating wiretapping and electronic surveillance. (See Blakey, "Aspects of The Evidence Gathering Process. Organized Crime Cases: A Preliminary Analysis," *Task Force Report on Organized Crime, President's Commission on Law Enforcement and Administration of Justice* 80 (1967)). In 1968, I was also the Reporter for the American Bar Association's Standards Relating to Electronic Surveillance (*ABA Project on Standards For Criminal Justice, Standards Relating to Electronic Surveillance* (March 1971)), and a special counsel to Senator John L. McClellan, when he introduced and secured the passage of Title III on wiretapping and electronic surveillance of P.L. 90–351 (18 USC § 2510 *et. seq.*). Those of us involved in the work of the Crime Commission, the ABA Project, and the Congress argued that those involved in the administration of justice needed access to modern evidence-gathering tools and that the quantity and quality of the evidence available to courts and juries would be substantially enhanced by the adoption of techniques of electronic surveillance. (See, for example, *ABA Standards* at 126 ("[E]very effort should be made to record . . . conversations through the best possible means. For a recording will reproduce the very words spoken with all the added significance that comes from inflection, emphasis and the other aspects of oral speech . . . The goal of finding the truth in the criminal trial demands no less.")) In 1976, I was appointed by the President to the National Commission for the Review of Federal and State Laws relating to Wiretapping and Electronic Surveillance, which was created by PL 90–351 to study the implementation of Title III. We took extensive testimony from law enforcement personnel, prosecutors, defense counsel, and judges actively engaged in the administration of justice throughout the United States on the federal and state levels. All agreed that recorded conversations made under the 1968 Act of defendants engaged in various crimes made a "strong, if not indelible, impression on jurors" (*Report* at 132). The witnesses who testified before us described tapes as "among the most reliable and accurate evidence that exists" and "the most powerful evidence that the prosecution can offer in a criminal case." (*Id.*) (One defense attorney told us that defendants wanted to "hide under the table when they hear themselves talking." (*Id.*)) They also testified that such evidence broadened the scope of prosecutions and enabled deeper penetration by the government of hierarchical criminal organizations. The presence of tapes, they thought, was also a significant factor in the decision of a defendant to plead guilty. Indeed, they testified that in criminal prosecutions based on tapes, defendants tended to be more honest with their lawyers, prosecutors tended to be more candid with defendants and their counsel, and both tended to be more forthright with the court and jury. As a result, they testified, "fewer spurious prosecutions or defenses, credibility contests, and jury issues" occurred in a criminal trial where the participants had access to tapes of the crucial conversations. (*Id.* at 133.) Finally, they testified that such evidence had a beneficial impact on the defendant himself in his acceptance of his own culpability and made it easier for him to come to terms with his own guilt. Tapes, in short, made "the evidence . . . there for all to see and hear . . . [and] the facts and the consequences . . . clear to all." (*Id.*)

In 1981, the Senate Permanent Subcommittee on Investigations, as a culmination of a year-long probe, held two weeks of hearings on corruption and organized crime domination of the waterfront on the east coast of the United States (*Waterfront Corruption*: Hearings before the Perm. Subcommittee on Investigations, Comm. on Government Affairs, 97th Cong., 1st Sess. (1981)). The evidence reviewed by the Committee was the result, not only of its own efforts, but of a five-year investigation by the Federal Bureau of Investigation that included the use of more than 1100 hours of electronic surveillance tapes, undercover activities, and grant jury proceedings. The evidence revealed a pervasive and sordid pattern of payoffs, kickbacks, threats, and obstruction of justice on the waterfront from New York City to Miami, Florida. A "racketeering tariff" was added to every service or product moved in commerce by the shipping industry, making American goods less competitive and American ports more costly. The victims included members of unions, who placed their trust in their leadership, the stockholders of companies, whose money was unlawfully paid out, and the American people, who paid higher prices for goods. FBI Director William Webster termed the investigation "the most successful labor racketeering investigation ever conducted by the FBI." (*Id.* at 8) In particular, the Senate hearings traced the rise and fall of Anthony Scotto, from the day, at age 28, he pledged loyalty to organized crime boss Carlo

Gambino, for which he was made a member of the Gambino crime family, ultimately a *caporegima* or captain in the family, and the president of Local 1814 of the International Longshoreman Association, to the day he was indicted under the Organized Crime Control Act of 1970. As a result of his pledge of loyalty to Gambino and his rise in the union, Scotto acquired significant political power on the local, state, and national level. Scotto's position at the time of his trial was well-illustrated by his character witnesses: Governor Hugh Carey of New York, former New York City Mayors John Lindsey and Robert Wagner, and then Secretary -Treasurer, now President of the AFL-CIO, Lane Kirkland. According to testimony in the hearings, Scotto's conviction was made possible through the use of electronic surveillance. Jack Burnett, the principal FBI agent on the investigation, called it the "single most important tool." (*Id.* at 233) After closing statements, in which the prosecutor argued that "Scotto's own voice" on the tapes was the best evidence of his "greed, power and corruption" (New York Times, Nov. 10, 1979, p. 25, col. 5), the jury declined to accept Scotto's defense that he received the payments as campaign contributions for Mario M. Cuomo, then a mayoral candidate in New York City, now the Governor of New York, and the then Governor of New York, Hugh Carey; it also appropriately discounted Scotto's impressive character testimony. Juror Lucille Brockway later observed: "Most of us thought . . . [the campaign contribution defense] was a cock-and-bull story – I called it a fairy tale day the first time it came up in court" (New York Times, Nov. 17, 1979, p. 27, col. 5). The jurors emphatically cited the tapes as the key to their decision, and they commented that the character witnesses' unfamiliarity with what they so amply demonstrated greatly detracted from their testimony. Brockway summed up their decision: "The tapes were crucial [:it was] the hardest evidence." (*Id.*)

The average juror, however, is not always able to understand what he or she hears on a tape. When John Gotti, the successor head of the Gambino family, refers on a recorded conversation to a *"rappresentante"* or a *"consigliere"* (*The Gotti Tapes* 74 (1992) ("head of family" and "counsellor")), these words, spoken in the argot of the underworld, must be explained to the jury by an expert witness, whose testimony is a familiar feature of modern organized crime prosecutions. (See, for example, *United States v. Riccobene*, 709 F.2d 214, 230–1 (3rd Cir.), ("La Cosa Nostra," "*capi*," "*consigliere*" properly explained by expert testimony), *cert. denied*, 464 US 849 (1983)). Similarly, when the prosecution is of loansharks or other organized crime figures, expert testimony must often be introduced, so that the jury can understand the specialized language and practices characteristic of that particular form of criminal endeavor. (See, for example, *United States v. Vostola*, 899 F.2d 211, 232–4 (3rd Cir. 1990) (police officer's testimony on the meaning of "coded" loansharking conversations upheld), *vacated on other grounds*, 110 S. Ct. 3233, *aff'd and rev'd in part on other grounds on remand*, 915 F.2d 865, *conviction reinstated*, 772 F. Supp. 1472 (DC NJ 1991); *United States v. Barletta*, 565 F.2d 985, 991–2 (8th Cir. 1977) (FBI expert in "ways and language" of bookmakers permitted to interpret recorded "ambiguous conversation"); *United States v. Ruggiero*, 928 F.2d 1289, 1304–5 (2nd Cir.) (operations of narcotics dealers proper subject of expert testimony; admission of testimony concerning meaning of recorded conversations upheld), *cert. denied*, 112 S. Ct. 372 (1991).)

Unfortunately, appellate decisions are not always as hospitable as they should be to the introduction of the expert testimony of a linguist such as Shuy, on the interpretation of oral conversations. (See, for example, *United States v. Evans*, 910 F.2d 790, 802–4 (11th Cir. 1990) (not an abuse of discretion to exclude Dr Shuy's linguistics testimony), *aff'd on other grounds*, 112 S. Ct. 1881 (1992); *United States v. Devine*, 787 F.2d 1086, 1088 (7th Cir.) (not an abuse of discretion to exclude Dr Shuy's auditory and phonetic testimony), *cert. denied*, 479 US 848 (1986); *United States v. Kupau*, 781 F.2d 740, 745 (9th Cir. 1986) (not an abuse of discretion to exclude Dr Shuy's linguistics testimony) (citing *United States v. Schmidt*, 711 F.2d 595, 598–9 (5th Cir. 1983) (close question), *cert. denied*, 464 US 1041 (1984) and *United States v. Hearst*, 563 F.2d 1331, 1349–50 (9th Cir. 1977), *cert. denied*, 435 US 1000 (1978)).

A few appellate decisions, of course, seldom accurately reflect the general course of trial court practice. (See generally Note, "The Admissibility of Expert Testimony on the Discourse Analysis of Recorded Conversation," 38 U. of Fla. L. Rev. 69 (1986)). In fact, prosecutors show little awareness of the value of the testimony of linguists. More often, defendants seek to use it. If the linguist's testimony on behalf of a defendant is admitted, and the defendant is found not guilty, unless the issue is resolved in a pretrial proceeding, an appeal by the prosecution is precluded by the doctrine of double jeopardy; if the linguist's testimony is admitted, and defendant is convicted, the defendant cannot appeal the admission of the testimony of his own witness. Accordingly, appeals typically occur in this area only when the defendant is unsuccessful in introducing such testimony, and the defendant is convicted. More often than not, Shuy is permitted to testify, as *Language Crimes* well illustrates. Nevertheless, sometimes he is not permitted to testify and an appeal is taken. Reversal of a decision to exclude expert testimony, however, seldom occurs, since appellate review is conducted under the prevailing abuse of discretion standard, and it is subject to the harmless error doctrine. A trial court decision in such trials, on the other hand, turns on an evaluation of the relative degree of helpfulness of a linguist's testimony to the jury, where the "subject matter of the testimony, conversation, . . . [is] one which could be expected to be within the general knowledge of jurors," and where the possibility of "confusion" of the jury is taken into consideration. (See, for example, *Evans*, 90 F.2d at 803.)

Secondguessing a trial court solely on the basis of an appellate opinion is difficult, but few who read – nay study – *Language Crimes* will come away with the settled impression that the interpretation of oral conversations is, in fact, so clearly within the general competency of the average juror that such interpretation may safely be left to the jury with a tape and a transcript enlightened only by the arguments of single-minded advocates and the general instructions of the court. Agreement with Shuy's interpretation of each of the series of conversations that he sets out in *Language Crimes* or agreement – or disagreement – with each jury verdict he notes is not necessary to accord his testimony and his field of expertise their just due. In each instance, Shuy's analysis, based on the general insights of linguistics, is cogent, even if it is not necessarily decisive on the ultimate issue of guilt or innocence. The fundamental mistake, if any, occurs in a court too quickly excluding it, not in a jury discounting it in light of other evidence that points in another direction. I, for one, find it difficult, therefore, to justify these trial court decisions excluding Shuy's testimony. Truth would be better served if it were admitted.

Indeed, common experience itself convincingly argues for the use of a linguist's testimony in most contested prosecutions involving recorded oral communications. Oral communication, of course, works well enough for most practical purposes, particularly where participants help each other understand, and each is free to ask the other for clarification. Recorded oral conversations, however, are frozen in time. Subsequent clarifications in a trial are too often colored by the process itself. The point is not sophisticated: those of us who are happily married surely know how even a loving spouse, who can often know what we are going to say before we say it, sometimes misunderstands what was said or intended. How much more so may it be said of those tragic and unhappy relationships, where despite what is said, nothing is understood? Similarly, those of us with children – of all ages – know how difficult it is to communicate across generations, parent to child or child to parent. Even professionally, do law students always understand the clearest of lectures? Do law professors always understand the clearest of questions? Do associates in law firms always understand the most cogent of directions given by the most articulate of senior partners? Do law clerks – or even the litigants themselves – always understand what the judge tells them in open court in the clearest of language? Given the inherent limitations on accurate communication in oral conversation, the most remarkable aspect of oral communication is that so much is, in fact, successfully accomplished, not that so much miscommunication so often occurs.

When a man's or woman's life or liberty hangs in a delicate balance on an issue so troublesome as the meaning of language, the objective of increasing the quantity and quality of evidence available to juror and court is frustrated if efforts to implement it are not accompanied by making available to juror and court the best linguistics expertise possible for assistance in interpreting the meaning of the tapes. The goal of finding the truth in the criminal trial here too demands no less. If Shuy's *Language Crimes* helps to enlighten the attitude of those members of the trial bench, whose tendency is to assume that the linguist's testimony is not helpful, since it is only "oral conversation," and moves them to make available to jurors and themselves the insights

2

of linguistics, then his contribution to the administration of justice will be, in its own way, as significant as the enactment of Title III itself was in 1968.

G. Robert Blakey
William and Dorothy O'Neil
Professor of Law
Notre Dame Law School
Notre Dame, Indiana

Introduction:
New Directions

In the early summer of 1979 I was sitting in the middle seat on an airplane on my way to an academic meeting in Dallas. Next to me sat a gentleman who was intently reading a manuscript. Since it was quite possible for me to read his text, I noticed that it appeared to be a sermon. Several minutes passed, the plane took off, levelling at 25,000 ft, and the stewardesses began serving dinner. In the ritual of conversation on airplanes, it is generally understood that one of the times that passengers can begin conversations is when food is served. So I broke the ice: "I couldn't help noticing that you were reading a sermon. Are you a minister or priest?" "No," he replied, "I'm an attorney representing a television evangelist in a lawsuit." He volunteered a great deal more about his case, explaining that the suit had been brought by the evangelist against a TV station that had prohibited him from preaching against homosexuality. It was a Federal Communications Commission matter and he specialized in such cases. He then asked me what my field of work was and I explained that I was a linguist who specialized in language variation. I recounted my years of experience in tape recording interviews with hundreds of Americans so that I could document the regional and social dialects of American English. Suddenly the attorney's eyes lit up, "Tape-recorded data?" "Yes," I replied, "it's called sociolinguistics."

The attorney then quickly shifted his focus away from the matter involving the evangelist to a different case, one in which a colleague of his, Richard "Racehorse" Haynes, was the lead defense attorney. He told me that law enforcement officers had made surreptitious recordings of several conversations of a certain Texas millionaire who was accused of soliciting the murder of his wife and the judge in his divorce trial. He wanted to tell his colleague about me and maybe they would send me the tapes to review. I agreed and thought no more about it until a week or two later, when I got a telephone call from Sam Guiberson, a lawyer working with Richard "Racehorse" Haynes. Guiberson told me that he had originally suggested using a linguist in the case and that I might be exactly the person they were looking for.

I agreed to review the tapes but when I first listened to them I was thoroughly shocked. I had never heard a discussion about killing people before and it frightened me a great deal. Nevertheless, I listened to the tapes over and over again and finally realized that both men weren't discussing killing people; that only one of the men was doing this. Additional listening made it clear, furthermore, that the man who was not discussing the murders was not really responding to the other man, who always introduced that topic. I wasn't sure what this all meant but I reported my observations to Guiberson and he explained that I had unlocked an important key to the case. Guiberson and Haynes never did explain to me their theory of the case but they gave me every encouragement to proceed along the lines I had outlined to them.

As a result, I developed a theory of conversational contamination, a concept that I have used many times since. Conversational contamination means only that when we overhear two people talking, telling an ethnic joke, for example, we tend to assume that both parties are doing the telling, that both parties are equally guilty of generating the story. But in order to really understand this joke-telling event, we need to know who introduced the topic and what response the listener made. The whole event cannot be captured by the words of only one participant. Suppose, for example, the listener says nothing at all? Suppose he says only "Uh-huh"? Does this mean that he is an active participant? That he shares the stigma of telling the ethnic story? That he even appreciates the joke? Does he give away any clues to his not appreciating it? Does he appear to be uncomfortable, wishing perhaps that he were somewhere else?

With these thoughts in mind I decided to do a topic analysis of the conversations. This procedure would indicate exactly who brought up which topics. If our client was guilty of soliciting murder, he might be expected to have at least introduced the subject at some point during the tape-recorded conversations. The topics that people bring up are one important clue to what is on their minds, what their conversational agendas are. There is no way a linguist (or anyone else, as far as I know) can penetrate the minds of speakers and determine what their exact intentions actually are. But when there is a tape recording of the event in question, we have access to important clues to such intentions, just as fragments of pottery can give archeologists clues about ancient civilizations. Likewise, the types of responses given to substantive topics provide clues to the intentions of the persons who respond. They too give strong indications of their state of mind, their intentions, their conversational agendas.

Language Crimes brings together a number of actual cases in which I served as an expert witness or consultant. The intention of these accounts is to point out the importance of linguistic analysis for resolving law cases in which language is the major, if not the only, evidence offered by the prosecution. I have worked on behalf of a number of nationally known public figures, entertainers, politicians, industrial giants. I have also worked on behalf of the little guys, those who are relatively obscure but whose stories are every bit as significant and compelling.

In the following chapters, I describe some of the ways in which linguists approach tape-recorded evidence in criminal law cases. Since linguistics is virtually invisible to most people, I begin with the many misconceptions about language that most people (such as jurors but, in many cases, also attorneys) bring with them in their encounters with evidence in the form of tape-recorded conversations. Just as physicians are trained to see things in an X-ray that the average person with excellent vision cannot see, so linguists are trained to see and hear structures that are invisible to lay persons.

Judges who may be skeptical about whether or not to allow a linguist to testify in a given case are often concerned about why a jury might be helped by linguistic analysis. Prosecutors regularly proclaim that it does not take such expertise to hear and understand a conversation. One such prosecutor recently asked me, in fact, whether I had had my hearing checked recently. His focus, of course, was on the wrong thing. A linguist's hearing may be no better than a juror's hearing, but the linguist's *listening* skills are finely honed by training and experience. Listening goes beyond hearing. It involves finding the patterns that exist in language. It includes attending to the many things that average listeners overlook when they hear speech. It requires consciously attending to the "little" things that most people ignore as they try to understand the "big" things they hear.

Native speakers know their language so well that they filter out all the tools of phonology, morphology, syntax, and discourse that they subconsciously use to make meaning out of what is said in their presence. Analogies can be found in many other areas of human existence, such as balance and vision. The complex rules of physics that govern our ability to walk or to ride a bicycle are never in the minds of human beings as they perform these operations; but physical laws of optics, light, perspective and the physical universe operate nonetheless. A specialist in physics can find them; a walker or bike-rider calls on these laws without any conscious awareness of having used them. To understand the act of walking or bike-riding, we need the physicist to "listen" and describe what is going on in much the same way that we need a linguist to listen and describe the structure of a conversation. The average layman can hear what is obvious on the surface but is considerably less able to listen for the meaning that is present in the contextual clues of language. Just like the physicist in the example above, linguists know what to listen for in a conversation. They listen for topic initiations, topic recycling, response strategies, interruption patterns, intonation markers, pause lengths, speech event structure, speech acts, inferencing, ambiguity resolution, transcript accuracy and many other things. Scientific training enables linguists to categorize structures that are alike and to compare or contrast structures that are not. Linguists understand the significance of context in the search for meaning in a conversation and are unwilling to agree with interpretations wrenched from context by either the prosecution or the defense.

Following the chapter on public misconceptions about language, I describe the speech event of bribery. There is a predictable structure to such an event just as there is a predictable structure in the speech event of the medical interview, the classroom interaction, or the everyday task of making a purchase (what linguists call a service encounter). The significance of describing bribery event structure is that the event structure serves as a kind of template against which any accusation of bribery can be measured.

If the conversation captured on tape is a true bribery event, that conversation should include the essential structural units of the bribery event.

The remaining chapters deal primarily with the speech acts of offering, agreeing, threatening, admitting, lying, promising and requesting. Speech acts are, quite simply, the ways that people use language to get things done. Since resolution of many criminal cases hinges on whether or not the accused person actually offers, agrees, threatens, admits, lies, promises or requests, accurate identification of these speech acts is, to say the least, crucial. The Model Penal Code provides the basis for my use of speech acts as the organizing principle of this book.

Linguistic analysis offers the field of law some principled ways of making such accurate identifications, relieving the jury of the necessity of having to guess at such matters. Linguistic analysis offers jurors ways of viewing the evidence that will help them see the language structures that are there, on the tape, but difficult for the lay person to see or hear, without the specific training or experience to consciously or systematically do this kind of thing.

To my colleagues in linguistics I would like to point out that this is not intended to be a linguistics textbook. I have written for a broader audience, particularly for those who have little or no background in linguistics. For this reason, I have tried to be as non-technical as possible, much as I would talk in the actual courtroom. Appearing as an expert witness may well be the ultimate test of the applied linguist, since we are expected to be technically expert enough to have useful things to tell the jury but, at the same time, effective enough as teachers to be able to communicate technical information in ways that can be of immediate interest and usefulness to a jury.

As they ponder whether or not to permit a linguist to testify in a given case, judges seem to be very concerned that what the expert witness has to say will be too technical and complex for a jury to comprehend. The paradox here is that if the linguist is so clear and non-technical that the information presented seems to be little more than common sense, the judge may deem the testimony unnecessary. Obviously a middle ground is called for. But this middle ground is actually no different from a good definition of teaching, in which new or complex information is effectively introduced in well-presented stages or increments, is well illustrated with listener-friendly examples and is accompanied by visual charts. I have found that listeners are apt to be convinced by what they hear but they tend to remember better what they see. For this reason I usually accompany my courtroom testimony with charts that illustrate or summarize what I say on the witness stand.

Over the past dozen years or so, since I first met the attorney on the airplane who introduced me to "Racehorse" Haynes and Sam Guiberson, I have consulted on over 200 criminal and civil cases and have been admitted as an expert witness in some 35 trials, despite the constant objection of prosecutors.

Rule 702 of the Federal Rules of Evidence says the following:

> If scientific, technical, or other specialized knowledge will assist the trier of fact to understand the evidence or to determine a fact in issue, a witness qualified as an expert by knowledge, skill, experience, training or education, may testify thereto in the form of opinion or otherwise.

Under Rule 702, the test for admissibility of such testimony has three tests:

1 Whether the discipline of linguistics is grounded in sufficient scientific, technical or other specialized knowledge to warrant its use in the courtroom.
2 Whether the proposed linguist-witness is a qualified expert in this discipline.
3 Whether the application of linguistic analysis to the evidence in the case will assist the jury in understanding that evidence or in determining a fact in issue.

In the few instances when a judge has not permitted my testimony, the court did not state that my proffered testimony was legally inadmissible, nor did it contest the scientific validity of linguistics as a discipline or my status as an expert. The only concern expressed by any court was whether or not the jury might be assisted by such testimony. This is, of course, a judgment call by the judge, who can decide this issue in several ways. The court can hear my testimony outside the presence of the jury and then make a decision. Or the court can listen to the attorney's representation of what the linguist's testimony will be and decide on that basis. Or the court can review motions made by the defense and prosecution that may include representations about what the linguist will say and then decide on that basis. Whichever procedure is followed, the court has the right to decide to admit or deny my testimony. Neither decision is necessarily the basis for appeal since the court is making a judgment call.

The reader will probably notice that in all of the cases described here, my work was for the defense. Prosecutors try to make much of this during the trials in which I provide expert witness. My services have been used by the United States Department of Justice on two occasions but in neither case was I asked to provide expert witness testimony. I analyzed the tape recordings used as evidence for the prosecution in these cases, in exactly the same way that I would have analyzed them for the defense, had the defense attorneys called on me to do so. I can only speculate why the prosecution so infrequently calls on the services of linguists. There may be budget constraints, sheer confidence that the prosecution will prevail without the aid of linguistic analysis, unfamiliarity with the resources available, lack of time, or any number of possibilities. One unspoken reason may be that if the prosecution were to use a linguist at trial, this event would legitimize the use of linguists to the courts and defuse many objections that prosecutors may wish to make for the defense's use of a linguist in the future.

But one thing should be very clear. Linguistic analysis in criminal or civil cases is utterly unrelated to either the defense or the prosecution. Linguists analyze language, not guilt or innocence. The same analysis should emerge whether it is done for the defendant or the prosecution. We can't change the language on a tape. In fact, on many occasions after reviewing tapes sent to me by defense attorneys, best advice is for the attorney to take whatever plea bargain he can get. In some cases, there is little or nothing that anybody can do for the defendant anyway.

During his unsuccessful effort to be confirmed as a Justice in the United States Supreme Court, Judge Robert Bork uttered a phrase which I, as an academic, found apt and attractive but which came back to haunt him during his confirmation hearing process. When asked why he wanted to be a Supreme Court Justice, Bork said that he viewed the job as "an intellectual feast."

I find that each case I accept is an intellectual feast layed out before me. For an academic, the conventional intellectual feast involves thinking through an abstract problem or theory, conducting a scientific analysis, surveying any issue in one's field or simply reading what others have said. In a court case, abstraction comes crashing into reality. Human lives are at stake and the results of my analysis can have tangible and immediate significance. The problem I address is not an artificial or theoretical one. I maintain that if linguistics has meaning at all, it should have meaning in such a real world. Years of research, theorizing and categorizing should be applicable to the here and now of daily living. The problem presented by each court case is, in itself then, a kind of intellectual feast.

When I told the attorney sitting next to me in 1979 that I had tape recorded hundreds of Americans in order to analyze their speech patterns, I little suspected that from that point on, my research would change so dramatically. For example, I no longer need to go to the field and conduct tape-recorded interviews for my speech samples. Law enforcement agencies do it for me, providing the table for the intellectual feast of analysis and presentation.

Note

Before 1982, FBI investigations were given code names which related to the nature or subject of the operation. Thus, "Abscam," referred to in this book, stood for "Arab scam" and "Brilab" was short for "bribery of labor unions." In 1982, the Congressional committee charged with overseeing the FBI recommended that all future operation names should have no particular significance. An FBI investigation of Chicago attorneys and judges, which followed shortly after this recommendation, was named operation Greylord. Although some observers have speculated that this referred descriptively to judges (in the historical British sense of wigs and gowns), the real origin of the name is far less exciting: it was named after a racehorse which was running at Arlington Race Track in the Chicago area.

1

Misconceptions about Language in Law Cases

As far as I can tell, nobody has ever been indicted or convicted for thanking someone for something or for apologizing for a thoughtless act or statement. Crimes are reserved for other types of language use, including threatening, offering a bribe, extorting, or soliciting things like murder or illicit sex. These and other acts are accomplished through language, not through physical acts. For this reason, the field of law must rely on what is known about how language works in order to evaluate legal evidence which just happens to be in the form of language.

Many people, when presented with the words "language crimes" think immediately of their pet indiscretions against standard English. But we are not talking here about such things as ending sentences with prepositions, using "contact" as a verb, or the overuse of the common expression, "you know." Although such phrases are frowned upon, they do not lead to criminal indictments or trials. In contrast, when one person threatens another, that threat can lead to litigation. Something as simple and harmless as an offer can also lead to a criminal trial if the offer is for something that it is not legal to accomplish. Likewise, one can solicit or request something quite legally. But if one solicits or requests certain things, such as the murder of one's wife or sexual favors from a prostitute, one is committing a crime through language alone. One does not actually need to do harm to the person threatened, give the bribe, have the wife killed, or engage in sex with the prostitute. The language threat, offer, or solicitation is enough to constitute a crime.

However obvious the above may seem, it is not generally re-cognized that the use of language can be so closely associated with criminality. The general public tends to conceive of crime in terms of physical acts such as stealing, killing, molesting, or hurting another person, the widely recognized crimes of violence. We fear these things, and it is not surprising that they should be foremost in our consciousness.

Traditionally, persons who have been injured, robbed, or molested accuse someone of such acts and report what they have seen and experienced to the police and in the trial court. Like-wise, persons who are accused report what they believe to be true about the event. Witnesses, if any, also report what they believe to have happened. All of this, of course, takes place in the form of language. But all this language has one thing in common – it reports memories and perceptions of past events – it does not comprise the events themselves. As remembered reports, they are, of course, subject to all the failures of recall, misunderstanding, and misperception of human life. Elizabeth Loftus, among others, has provided many important insights into the difficulties of eye-witness evidence (see her *Eyewitness Testimony*, Harvard Uni-versity Press, 1979).

Whatever problems may arise when memory and perception of physical events involving crimes are concerned, such problems can be multiplied when a language crime is suspected. The same problems of memory, understanding, and perception are there but to these we now must add the clues to intention that language offers. Not only must jurors consider the words that were said, for example, in a tape-recorded conversation that is used as evi-dence in a criminal case, but also they must consider the context in which these words were said, the several possible meanings provided by imperfect, inexplicit, vague word selection, the social roles of the participants, and many other factors.

On the surface, this may seem to be a rather easy thing for a juror to do. But it is not easy at all. For one thing, the average person begins the task of listening to tape-recorded conversation of other people with a number of preconceptions about the event being recorded and, very significantly, about language itself. Such preconceptions can easily lead to misconceptions if the juror is not very careful.

Misconceptions about defendants

1 If they are on tape at all, they must be guilty of something; otherwise the police would not have been after them.
2 If they are guilty of one of the charges, they are probably guilty of the other charges as well.
3 The defendants hear, understand, and remember everything said by the agent or other persons in the taped conversation.

These three misconceptions, individually or together, can lead to a gross misunderstanding of any conversation being examined. We need look no farther than to conversations in which we have been involved ourselves. Suppose somebody recorded us at a party when we were cornered by a person we do not particularly like. That person insists on telling us an off-color joke. What we might *like* to do is to tell that person that the joke is inappropriate or insulting, but social constraints, personal weakness or sheer indifference cause us to go along with it, laugh politely and try to excuse ourselves from that person as quickly as possible. Then, later on in the evening, the person who secretly taped the incident plays it back and observes that we were *all* telling dirty jokes. "No!" We object. "*We* were not telling dirty jokes, *John* was." But the objection falls on deaf ears. The tape speaks for itself. We laughed. We went along with it. We didn't object. We didn't turn and walk away. We were there; therefore we were as guilty as the man who told the joke. The person who taped the conversation must have suspected how we would react. Otherwise he wouldn't have taped it.

The police and other government agencies who decide to surreptitiously tape record people have their own reasons for doing so. Often, their suspicions are justified, but sometimes they are not. Such occasions are mere tests, fishing expeditions, or attempts to expand an existing network of evidence to include other people. At worst, the agency may simply be trying to catch "a big fish" to justify the expense of an investigation that had, to that point, netted only petty crooks.

It has been claimed by prosecutors in tape cases that "the tapes speak for themselves," and that "all the jury has to do is listen to the tapes and they can easily determine what they say." This is in one sense quite true but, in another sense, *not* an easy thing to do. Often the jurors must listen to a great many tapes of a number of speakers talking to different people about various topics over long periods of time. Simply keeping the thread of conversation straight is no easy task. Keeping the context straight is even more difficult. Deciding on the meaning of ambiguous statements is monumentally troublesome.

Add to this the fact that the agent who wears the body microphone has one major goal – to capture, on tape, the target's involvement in a language crime. The target's mere presence in that conversation is not evidence enough but when a tape is presented as evidence of criminality, those who listen to it easily forget this fact.

Citizens have a justifiable belief that the police, the FBI, postal inspectors and other government agencies have good reason to suspect targets of investigation. Such a belief, however justifiable, is made subject to suspicion, however, whenever that agency goes beyond its factual intelligence information and slips into the role of "fishing for others." How many times have we been in a conversation when someone goes into great detail to tell us something that is of little concern to us? We ask ourselves, "Why is he telling me this?" We have our own concerns, our own conversational agendas and this person's topic is so far off our base that we tend to ignore it, discount it and soon forget it.

But suppose that person was telling us about an illegal act he had committed or was thinking about committing. Do we believe him? Do we attempt to dissuade him? Do we even *hear* him? Conversation is guided, as the language philosopher H. P. Grice has indicated, by several principles, or maxims, one of which is the maxim of relevance (see his "Logic and conversation" in P. Cole and J. Morgan (eds), *Syntax and Semantics 3*, Academic Press, 1976). People hear that which is relevant; they focus on it and organize what they hear around it. They have frames of reference (what psychologists call *schemas*) which cause them either to hear non-relevant topics in ways that are relevant to their own schemas or to sort them out as irrelevant, perhaps not even hearing them, but certainly not retaining them in memory. As we hear this person talk about an illegal event, we have to make a number of rapid adjustments, even if we listen carefully. Is he serious or joking? Is he just trying to shock us? Can the statement be categorized along with utterances like, "I'd kill my wife if she didn't do the dishes." Just where does the proper meaning really fall?

The second misconception is equally common. The "all or none" logical fallacy can work either for or against a defendant. I have seen defendants judged innocent of all charges when the taped evidence argued strongly for guilt on one or more charges but not all of them. But, more commonly, I have seen defendants found guilty of all charges when the evidence was clear on only one. The jury system is imperfect, but it is still the best thing we have.

This "all or none" problem exists for all types of criminal cases but it seems to be exacerbated where language crimes are the focus. In the example above, for instance, the person who tape recorded the dirty joke conversation might well hear and recall the incident as *all* of us telling dirty jokes. This is a classic example of the contamination principle of language. Those who listen to recordings of people talking tend to overgeneralize many things. For example, in the tapes involved in the case of Senator Harrison A. Williams Jr, (discussed in chapters 2 and 8) careful listening makes it clear that swearing on the tapes is being done overall by the government agents and by other participants, but *not* by Senator Williams. By the same token, the government operatives use the words *hidden interest*. Senator Williams uses the words *blind trust*. In a very few instances, the government agents use the words *government contracts*. Senator Williams does not. The words used by the government operatives about Senator Williams in the first meeting with the presumed Arab sheik contrasts sharply with what Senator Williams actually says about himself. Despite these clear contrasts in who said what, the court and even the US Senate Ethics Committee became victims of contamination and overgeneralized meanings which were not there. The principle of contamination is especially dangerous and unfair. Careful analysis of who said what in the actual recorded evidence is carried out by linguists to defuse and dispell this contamination.

Likewise, in the case of Congressman John Murphy, overt criminal acts (what I refer to as language crimes) occur only on tapes in which Murphy is not present. Money was exchanged between Angelo Errichetti and an FBI agent in the case of Kenneth

McDonald, but careful viewing of the video tape shows McDonald looking out of the window on the opposite side of the room (see chapter 3). He was clearly *not* a part of the conversation and not involved in what Errichetti and the agent were talking about.

In the jury's overall memory of the Williams, Murphy and McDonald tapes, it is precariously easy for jurors to be contaminated by confusing who was present and who was not, who suggested the illegal acts and who did not, and whether what was said was said *to* the target, or to someone else entirely. To confuse these important conversational tasks is to be contaminated by the taped evidence, or to be contaminated by the presentation of that evidence by one or both sides.

The written transcript of a tape-recorded conversation can also create listener contamination. The written transcript cannot possibly present all of the important information that the actual tape provides. Transcripts collapse time, making events appear immediate when, in fact, long pauses may have taken place. Transcripts do not usually show interrupted or overlapped speech, which is particularly important when more than one conversation is recorded at the same time. Transcripts do not show stressed words, a vital indication to the intentions of a speaker.

Furthermore, it has been my experience that government transcripts are almost always inaccurate in many places, by including misattribution of the speaker, by the addition of words *not* on the tape, by the deletion of words that *are* on the tape and by errors in representation of words on the tape. Almost invariably, crucial judgments must be made by jurors in areas where government transcripts are in error. In the Murphy and Thompson cases, crucial controversy hinged on whether or not the words "for me" were present in the target's sentence, "Take care of this." In the Senator Williams case, the transcript shows Williams saying "aye" to a motion made by the middle man, but his voice is not on the tape at that point.

The third misconception about defendants, that the target actually heard, understood, and remembered everything said by the agent or other persons in the tape-recorded conversation, is also dangerous. In the celebrated FBI operation in Chicago, called Greylord, various attorneys and judges were taped in their chambers and in their courtrooms. The general image of a judge's chambers, held by most people, is quite different from the offices of traffic court justices in many large cities. Many people come and go, shout and scream, engage in multiple topics at the same time. The fact that an agent says something that the microphone can record is clearly no guarantee that the target, or for that matter anyone else, could hear. But it is on tape and becomes reflected in the transcript of that tape. If the judge's voice can be heard at all, his next words also are recorded by the microphone and reflected on the transcript. If that judge happens to say "yes" to a bailiff's question about whether or not he wants a cup of coffee and that "yes" happens to occur after the agent simultaneously asks the question: "Would you take a $100 to fix a fine?" the tape recorder will pick up the agent's voice, not the bailiff's, and the judge will appear, to later listeners such as juries, to have agreed to a bribe.

Law is a culture of the written word, not the spoken. Once jurors see a written transcript, they think of it in the way they might view a written play. One actor says one thing and the next actor responds to that person with clear understanding, complete recall and perfect hearing. In real life, however, stage conditions do not exist. Lines are not memorized. The speakers do not have voices trained to carry to the last row of a theatre. Real people hear according to their schemas and overlook that which does not fit. Things get missed. Ideas are misunderstood. People come and go, often not even standing near each other. The distance that participants are from each other can be estimated from the sounds of their voices. In one case I worked on, the target's voice starts loud and gradually gets weaker throughout his sentence. This fading is accompanied by the sounds of footsteps. The agent's following statement is then uttered very softly. The statement was a crucial, incriminating one. Did the target even hear the agent? If one were to read the transcript only and not listen to the tape carefully, one would believe that there was a dyadic interaction. But when one listens to the tape, such an exchange seems highly improbable. Jurors who do not take these things into consideration run serious risks of misconception about the defendant.

They tend to assume guilt from the onset, rather than studying carefully the context of the conversation.

Misconceptions about language

1   Meaning is found primarily in individual words.
2   Listening to a tape once will be enough to determine its content.
3   Reading a transcript of a tape is as good as hearing the tape itself. Transcripts are accurate and they convey everything that is on the tape.
4   All people in a conversation understand the same things by their words.
5   People say what they mean and intend.

It would be convenient if these five points were true rather than misconceptions. Life would be simpler, if not duller. But meaning is conveyed in many ways besides words. Language is so complex and rapid that it goes by us too quickly for total processing. The written version of spoken language, however beautiful and useful it is for many purposes, simply does not reflect all the information conveyed by speech. People in conversations often do not understand the same things even though they hear the same words. And, since conversation is a social event as well as an information exchange event, people often say what social graces prescribe rather than what they really mean or want to say.

It is extremely dangerous to isolate anything from context, especially words. Consider the following conversation in a criminal case involving the alleged efforts of a Japanese industrial engineer to buy internal product secrets from an FBI agent posing as the representative of an American company:

Agent: You see, these plans are very hard to get.
Engr: Uh-huh.
Agent: I'd need to get them at night.
Engr: Uh-huh.
Agent: It's not done easily.
Engr: Uh-huh.
Agent: Understand?
Engr: Uh-huh.

It was alleged by the prosecutor in this case that the engineer understood from what the agent said that the act of obtaining these plans was illegal. Further, it was averred, the engineer gave his consent to the effort by saying "uh-huh." Several things are wrong with such an assertion. For one thing, the second guideline of the FBI states: "It must be made clear and unambiguous that the act proposed is illegal." Although to an American, the inference of illegality may be rather clear (largely from the words, "get them at night"), to a person from a different culture, the clarity is questionable. The staff may be reduced in size at night, or it may not be scheduled to do such tasks during the day.

Likewise, the engineer's use of "uh-huh" does not signal agreement, assent, or even knowledge of the event. It is the culture of the Japanese to be polite and agreeable. When they speak English, however faltering, they tend to nod agreement and say "yes" and "uh-huh" constantly, even where it is inappropriate to do so. Politeness and face count for more than resolution in that culture. In any case, the engineer's first three "uh-huh" responses cannot be agreement since the words presented by the agent presumably conveyed new information. There is no logical way to agree with new information, opinions, or many other acts of speech. For example, one cannot logically agree with the statement, "I really liked that movie." One has no right to agree to someone else's opinion. To agree one would have to say that he or she liked that movie also. These three "uh-huh" responses, therefore, are nothing more than feedback markers, words that acknowledge that one is listening or, on occasion, that one is understanding so far.

The last "uh-huh" response, to the agent's question, "understand" is more likely to convey agreement, but not even then with any certainty. The illegality in this case has not been "clearly and unambiguously" presented, particularly to a foreigner. In addition, this selected passage and elsewhere throughout all the tapes in all the conversations, the engineer says "uh-huh" to everything said by the agent, including many instances in which such a response is totally inappropriate, such as:

Agent: Hello. How are you?
Engr: Uh-huh.
Agent: (to colleague:) Joe, bring me some coffee.
Engr: Uh-huh.

The point here is that meaning is not communicated by individual words by themselves. No American baseball fan would

suspect murderous intent upon hearing "kill the umpire!" at a
Red Sox game. The context tells us otherwise. "Kill" does not
mean to make dead. It means something like a complaint about
the umpire's decision. But "I disagree" is too pretentious at a
ballgame. The social rules of such an event prescribe more colorful,
if not violent, imagery. And nobody is confused by it.

The second misconception about language, that listening to
the tape just once is adequate for understanding and memory, is
equally fallacious. Once the government decided to use tape recordings of conversation as evidence, it embarked on a totally
new kind of court procedure, one which most courts still do not
fully comprehend.

It is likely, due to the frequency of the practice of tape recording,
that many, if not most, criminal lawyers will get such a case
sooner or later. Most attorneys are ill prepared, in terms of specific training or experience, to present such a case effectively.
Since the tape recordings are of the language used in conversation, the government's evidence is of a totally different type
from that which they are used to.

Typically, trial lawyers have testimony to deal with – what
different people say they remember about what happened. From
a researcher's perspective, this second-hand type of data is the
least highly regarded. No self-respecting scientist would present
an academic paper which was based on the recollections of researchers on the phenomenon being studied. Instead, they meticu-
lously gather first-hand evidence, analyze it, and display it for
verification or counter-analysis in their reports. This distinction is
between what we call primary and secondary evidence. With the
advent of surreptitious tape-recorded evidence, the government
has moved into the research scientist's world. Primary data are
now the key – data which can be analyzed, subject to the scrutiny
of specialists who have long worked in the academic field which
studies such data. For attorneys, this is a different prospect; one
which requires a different kind of thinking, a different kind of
analysis, a different kind of preparation and a different kind of
courtroom presentation. One listening to the tape-recorded evidence is often all that the jury will get. There are many reasons
for this, not the least of which is time. Already crowded courts
do the best they can to get trials expedited quickly and efficiently.
Some tape cases have only one or two tape recordings to deal

with and several listenings are possible. But in the case of John DeLorean (see chapter 4), for example, there were over 60 audio and video recordings. Even one listening to all tapes involved a tremendous expenditure of courtroom time.

When an attorney sends me the tapes in his case, I listen to them over and over again. The first task is to correct (or create) an accurate transcript, one that includes everything humanly possible to hear. For tape recordings done with a body microphone, often in restaurants, automobiles or other noisy places, I will listen to certain parts of a tape as many as 50 times. Such effort is especially necessary when the participants in a conversation talk at the same time, interrupt each other, get excited, speak at some distance from each other, have speech impediments, peculiarities or dialects, use a foreign language some of the time, or when the government's recording quality is poor.

It has been argued by prosecutors that multiple listenings to the tape create a kind of unreality. The people who were *in* that conversation originally, they argue, only got to hear it once. In a sense, they are right. But the task of later listeners, whether it is the prosecution, the defense, the jury, or the linguistic consultant, is very different from the task of the person who was *in* that conversation. We are not that person and yet we have to reconstruct, as nearly as possible, what it was like to *have been* that person at that time – both target and agent. We have to try to walk in their shoes in order to construct hypotheses of what was in their minds.

Language goes by so fast and is so complex that the outsider who tries to reconstruct that event *must* listen to it several times. The principle is similar to that involved in written composition with students and teachers. Good writers do not really need to be able to talk about how they use language to construct their essays or fiction. Likewise, good teachers have learned to distinguish high-quality writing from mundane prose. If teaching were no more than the assignment of grades, quality writing would get A and poor writing D and that would be the end of it. But good teaching is more than evaluation. It requires teachers to assist writers to improve. This, in turn, requires them to be able to analyze with meaningful categories made up of labels or words. It requires many re-readings with suggestions about other alternative wordings. It necessitates a shared frame of reference and a set of tools and concepts with which to discuss the problems. Such tools include grammatical categories and discourse analysis concepts. Teachers are required to know *more* than their students if they are in any way to be helpful, or teach them.

Later listeners, including jurors, are in a position similar to that of the teacher. They *could* just give the tape a grade of guilty or not guilty, basing it on some intuitive gut feeling. But they *should* be able to know *why* they assigned such a grade. Obviously, so should prosecutors and defense attorneys. They *should* have in their tool box a set of analytical routines to apply to a conversation in order to justify (to themselves, at least) the grade they assigned.

When the grade assigned by jurors hinges on whether or not a loose pronoun actually referred to a specific person, the task becomes even more critical. When the grade assigned by the jurors depends upon who, indeed, actually introduced the incriminating topic, the jury had better have some way to discover this fact. When the grade assigned by the jury revolves around the contextual meaning of an "uh-huh" response, that jury had better understand the difference between affirmation and a feedback response.

One way to get over the tendency of spoken language to be so complex and so fast is to make use of outside expertise, in this case, the linguistic expert witness. The task of such an expert is, essentially, to analyze the tape outside the courtroom and to present the findings at the trial. Unfortunately, this requires the expert to be hired by either the prosecution or the defense. Whichever it is, the other side screams lack of objectivity and favoritism. This issue, of course, is inherent in the advocacy system but one wonders why it is not possible for such expertise to be employed in some more neutral capacity, perhaps by the court itself.

Another possible resolution is to try to teach the jury to analyze the tapes themselves. Such a procedure once happened to me in a bribery/conspiracy case in Newark. The judge seemed uncertain whether or not to permit me to testify about my analysis of the tapes in that case. Finally, he decided that I could not mention the specific case, but that I could teach the jury what kinds of things to listen for in the conversations. However good the idea may have been, I found it extremely difficult to communicate so much information in the trial context and I finished with a clear impression that I had not succeeded.

The answer to the problem created by the use of hours and hours of taped conversation as evidence remains unclear. Juries should be able to listen to the tapes many times (naturally they can do so during deliberation, but it is unclear how extensive such practice really is). Juries should have some kind of linguistic guidance in how to do this, but the methods are still unresolved. Perhaps the best answer is to use a linguist as an expert witness but, at this time, there are very few linguists available for this type of work, either by inclination or by training. The irony of it is that the tapes are listened to *many* times by the prosecution and, less so, by the defense. Why the jury, of all people, should be so restricted is a complex issue. The time of the trial issue is important but, upon reflection, it is an odd definition of justice. More depressing is the argument given by some defense attorneys who simply do not want the tapes heard any more than necessary – possibly because they fear that their clients are guilty or because they fear the jury will not understand and will be contaminated in the ways discussed earlier.

The third misconception, of transcript versus tape recording, is rampant in criminal law. As noted earlier, law is a literary culture. The written word takes precedence over the spoken, as evidenced by the use of court reporter's written transcripts over the oral proceedings of a trial or deposition. This literary predisposition causes attorneys, courts, and even intelligence analysts to move as quickly as possible to produce a written transcript of all oral presentations, including surreptitiously taped conversation of suspected criminals.

As an index or guide to such conversations, written transcripts can be useful. But even courts of law claim that transcripts are not the evidence; tape recordings are. Transcripts are usually permitted during jury deliberation, and jurors are permitted to follow transcripts while tapes are being played in court. As harmless as such practice may seem, the effect of the written word, accurate or inaccurate, in front of jurors causes them to hear on the tapes what they see on the printed page. It is not unusual for the prosecution and the defense to submit competing transcripts in a criminal case, the judge often deciding that it cannot be determined which one is accurate.

The point here is that tape-recorded intelligence is unlike other types of intelligence. As noted earlier, language goes by the listener very quickly and *many* listenings are absolutely necessary. A common procedure for addressing the odious task of multiple listenings is to produce a written transcript, to slow down the rapid oral process for analytical purposes. Another common procedure is to have a secretary prepare such a transcript, since secretaries often do dictation and are familiar with such practice. Still another common practice is to have the government representatives (agents, cooperating informants, etc.) go over the tape and transcript draft to correct it from their own perceptions of what occurred. As logical as such a procedure may seem, it is fraught with dangers of perceptual bias. People who participate in the taped events are actually less able to determine what is actually on the tape than are well-trained total outsiders to the event.

Defendants in criminal cases are no better able to analyze conversation after the event, simply because the average person does not have the meta-language to describe his/her own language. Likewise, agents or surrogate agents who are wearing the microphone are easily influenced in their listening by their goals in taping a suspected criminal in the first place. That is, they may think they hear the suspect utter a given word or phrase simply because it is their goal to capture such words on tape. In a Nevada case in 1981, the prosecution and the defense were at total odds about one crucial sentence:

> *Prosecution transcript*: I would take a bribe, wouldn't you?
> *Defense transcript*:   I wouldn't take a bribe, would you?

A simple machine analysis of this sentence could have made clear to the prosecution that syllable sequence argued for the defense transcript and against the prosecution's. Representing each syllable as a dash, the actual words on the tape were as follows:

$$\underline{\quad}\ \underline{\quad}\ \underline{\quad}\ \underline{\quad}\ \underline{\quad}\ \underline{\quad}, \ \underline{\quad}\ \underline{\quad}?$$

That is, the tape displayed six syllables with a junctural pause (comma) followed by two syllables, not the five–three sequence argued by the prosecution. This clearly indicates that the defense transcript was the accurate one.

The point here is that the evaluator of the intelligence offered

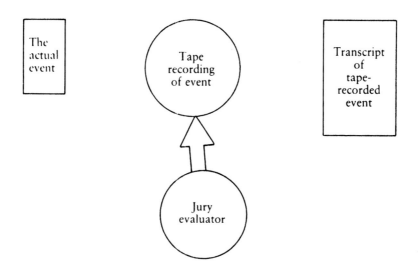

Figure 1.1   Evaluation of the tape, not the transcript.

by the tape had a schema in which the suspect said he would take a bribe. Therefore, the analyst heard it that way, despite the physical evidence to the contrary. The listener must not fall into the trap of overdependence on the written transcript of an oral event. Hours of painstaking effort must be spent on listening to the tape itself before a transcript is used at all. The transcript is *not* the evidence. It is, at best, only a weak representation of it or guide to the tape. Accurate evaluation should be made of the tape recording, not of the transcript of it, as figure 1.1 indicates.

There is a real danger in relying entirely on the written transcript of a conversation to determine exactly what is going on. Transcripts do not specify to whom a particular speech is intended or who has heard it. Assuming that transcripts are accurate in recording the words that were said (and they are often *not* accurate), they do not usually provide the important clues to conversation such as: *stress* (loudness), *intonation* (question marking versus statements), *pauses* (which carry their own form of meaning), *interrupting* (which can be a significant indication of speaker control and speaker intention), and many other things.

As defense attorneys try more and more tape cases, they are becoming increasingly aware of the principle of tape superiority to transcript both in their analyses of the evidence and in their courtroom presentations. It is therefore crucial that juries, prosecutors and defense attorneys rely on the tapes rather than the transcripts. Since transcripts are useful as points of reference, and for reporting purposes, it is equally important that they be as accurate as possible.

The fourth general misconception about language is that participants in a conversation understand the same things by the words that were spoken. For example, suppose a wife said to her husband, "The man came today." If there had been an earlier conversation about the need to call a plumber, her vague reference to "the man" might be predictable. On the other hand, without such a context, the husband might have some cause to be worried about just exactly who this man was.

Many people, including attorneys, have a naive but firm belief that language can be explicit and unambiguous. The truth is that language can only be *relatively* clear and explicit, simply because no two people share exactly the same experiences, feelings, and concerns. I define my house as clean and tidy if the floors are swept. Others may define a clean house as one with clean windows. I pay less attention to windows than floors. My uncle Roy inspected the house cleaning by running his fingers over the tops of picture frames. Unless they were dusted, his house wasn't clean. There is, in short, no way that language can account for all of the possible experiences and concerns that any two people can bring to a conversation. This is not to say that we cannot be somewhat clear or that we cannot avoid some ambiguities. Figure 1.2 shows one way to visualize these differences in comprehension of the same words.

The more alike two people are, the more they will have shared knowledge of the world, shared beliefs, shared feelings, shared concerns. But, as we said, even family members do not share all such knowledge. In much of life, ambiguous sentences result, usually brought about by incomplete statements or ambiguously uttered ones. Pronouns are the major culprit here. *They, he, she, it* and others are supposed to refer to specific, previously identified persons or things. But every day we engage in many conversations in which these pronouns are imperfectly referenced. When this happens, listeners are forced to infer the intended meaning and often they guess incorrectly, leading to a misunderstanding.

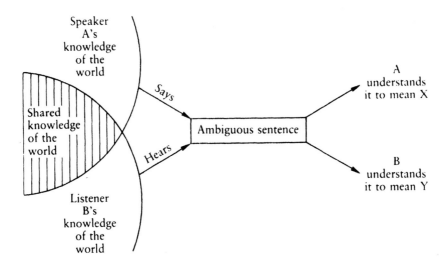

Figure 1.2   Differences in comprehension of the same words.

Sometimes one or both participants come to realize that something is wrong and the mistake is repaired. More often than not, however, the conversation goes on without either party understanding that two different meanings have evolved.

In a case involving a language crime, it is essential that such misunderstandings be noted if at all possible. The actual participants may have comprehended the same statement quite differently and the larger context of the conversation often makes clear that this is the case. If the jury is to "walk in the shoes" of the participants, it must be able to spot such ambiguities even though the participants may not have understood what was happening at the time of the actual event.

The fifth common misconception is that people say what they mean or what they really intend. The prosecutor's frequent claim, "the tapes speak for themselves," is not entirely true. The reason we often do not say what we mean has little or nothing to do with lying or evil intentions. It comes about simply because language is a social event, not just a cognitive one. There are socially accepted patterns of life, ones we have absorbed so fully and completely that we don't even know that we know them. We have already noted the maxim of relevance in conversation. People try to be relevant but, unfortunately, we define relevance differently. What seems very important to me may seem trivial or marginal to you. Role relationships also play an important role in conversation. We often hold back telling another person things that might disturb our concept of the propriety of our relationship. One of my graduate students for whom I have great fondness may not want to trouble me with facts about his deteriorating health, even though it affects the quality of his work. He deems it inappropriate to our role relationship. Physicians may not deem it necessary to correct their patients' misconceptions about anatomy on the grounds that their role is to heal, not to teach. An attorney may not see fit to correct a client's question, "How can I buy a pardon for my husband in prison?" deciding that the client has mis-spoken herself or that she is too upset to be given a lecture on the integrity of the legal system. But, if this conversation were tape recorded, the attorney would be criticized, if not indicted, as a willing conspirator in a plot to bribe an influential state senator.

The point here is that role relationships have a way of affecting a speaker to the extent that he may not choose to say what he really means. Politicians are particularly susceptible to this, as the FBI agents in the Abscam operation (see chapter 2) knew full well. What US senator would launch into a treatise on ethics and law to a presumed foreign dignitary who offers a bribe for assistance in getting into the USA? Of course, a bribe is illegal. But would this foreigner know American definitions of bribery? Would foreign relations be damaged by self-righteous indignation? Politicians get where they are by not offending, by being tactful, by avoiding confrontation. This, of course, makes them vulnerable to the kind of scenario posed in Abscam. Those who rejected the bribes, such as Senator Williams, did so, according to accusers, without moral indignation and disgust. Even though he rejected the bribe with a series of the word "no" and an explanation of why he could not accept money, the critics screamed "not good enough." But, as a politician, as a representative of one government to another, the social role of diplomacy did not permit indignation or disgust. He could not say what he meant.

Language crimes *are* committed with some regularity. People offer bribes, accept such offers, threaten people, extort them, perjure themselves and suborn perjury in others, solicit illegal things, slander, and libel people. Those who do so deliberately and illegally should be punished for breaking the law. If this were all there is to it, the job of the courts would be simple. As in most of life, however, serious problems arise in determining whether or not a bribe offer was actually made, or whether a solicitation really happened. The dimensions of these problems will be explored in the following chapters. All language crimes are subject to rigorous linguistic tests of authenticity, tests that distinguish a threat from a warning or distinguish acceptance of money designated as a campaign contribution from money designated as a bribe. In the rush of a single listening, in the clamor and excitement of a jury trial, and in the context of general misconceptions about language held by most people, language crimes can be very complex to identify and comprehend, and each one has its own story behind it.

2

Bribery

Bribery is one of the more common "white-collar" crimes. To most people, a bribe is self-evident: someone offers you money to do something that you should not do and you take the money and agree to do it. But bribery is much more complicated than this. Frequently, the offer of a bribe is mixed in with offers to do other legitimate things and the question becomes whether the person offered the bribe actually agrees to the legitimate or the illegitimate act. The nature of an offer is also complicated. Is it, for example, explicit or implied? That is, are the words in the offer so clear that no ambiguity results, as in: "I offer you $5,000." Or are the words used in such a way that the other person must guess at or infer that an offer is actually being made, as in: "I'd really like to help you with your problem."

An FBI agent who works undercover frequently faces a difficult problem when it is time to offer a target a bribe. To a Mafia figure, the agent may be able to use the word "bribe" directly in the offer on the assumption that bribery is standard procedure with such people. But even if he does not feel he can use the word "bribe," he can certainly be more direct than he would be to a corporate executive or a congressman. To such targets, the agent has to be more circumspect, so as to avoid insult. A natural companion of circumspection is indirectness, a more roundabout or suggestive use of language. When the agent is indirect in his offer, the target needs to infer (guess at) the intention and it is possible that he might guess wrong, leading to interminable disputes in any ensuing court trial about whether or not the suspect ever really understood the intent of the offer.

One way to determine whether or not a bribe event actually took place is to examine a number of instances in which a bribe is indisputably offered and accepted. Linguists commonly describe event structures, such as the structure of a doctor–patient interview or the structure of a sales event. Such structures describe the predictable elements of these events: how they begin, how they are resolved, conventions of participation, etc. After listening to dozens of surreptitious tape recordings of bribery events, it became clear to me that the successful bribe offer and acceptance contain four essential elements. Since these elements are sequenced, we shall call them phases. After conventional greetings and small talk are completed, the bribery event has the following phases: problem, proposal, completion, and extension.

Table 2.1 offers a model which accounts for all the conversations of this type in the body of data presented by the FBI as evidence in bribery cases. After the greetings phase, a problem is presented by the first party. It is usually a request for help of some sort. During this phase the first party checks on the other's authority and control to determine whether or not he or she is the appropriate person to follow up with a proposal. The next phase is the proposal itself, usually for services or products of some sort. Money is discussed and promises are made. Often at this phase, conditions are re-checked or new ones are introduced. If things are going well, some type of intimacy is established, often with anecdotes, stories about mutual friends and even with in-group language behavior. Both parties can engage in such checking and re-checking. Out of the proposal phase grows the completion phase, in which an offer is accepted, rejected, or deferred. If the offer is accepted, this is signaled by a handshake, the signing of an agreement, or verbal expressions such as "It's a deal." After the completion phase, there is usually a discussion about further extensions of the relationship now established, frequently involving other possible deals. This phase is followed frequently by extensive conventional closing.

Perhaps the most striking aspect of the structure of a bribe event is that it is identical to that of a business proposal event. It is, in fact, essentially the same structure that we use to purchase automobiles or to negotiate contracts. The only difference is in the nature of what attorneys call the quid pro quo: the legality of that which is offered and exchanged.

The structural similarity of a bribe event with a business proposal event becomes very important in criminal law cases for the

Table 2.1 Phases in the structure of a bribery event

Phases	Bribe offerer	Typical talk	Bribe receiver
Problem	Establish problem	Request help Check conditions and control of other party	Respond to problem
Proposal	Present offer	Service Products Payment Promises Money discussed	Consider offer Make conditions
	Re-check conditions, control, details	Establish intimacy with stories, in-group language	Re-check conditions, control, details
Completion	Complete contract offer	Handshake Contract "It's a deal"	Check conditions of offer Accept/reject offer
Extension	Extend business relationship	Plan other deals	Extend business relationship

business proposal structure, which seems common and natural to the person being offered a bribe, may actually help disguise what the briber actually intends. That is, a person who is not expecting to be bribed and who is offered the bribe indirectly, vaguely or not explicitly may not easily see that the event is an illegal proposition at all. Later listeners such as juries, however, listen with knowledge that was not available to the original target at the time of the offer. They now know clearly that a strong suspicion of bribery is present, that the government firmly believes that a bribe took place and that the tapes have the appearance of a bribe event.

But what exactly *is* this appearance? One of the most difficult tasks for a jury is to separate *appearances* from facts. "If it looks like a crime, it must be a crime," they might reason. The point here, however, is that appearances are not enough and both juries and prosecutors must learn to realize that the event structure may actually camouflage the legality of what is happening positively to the target and negatively to themselves.

The second striking aspect of the bribe event is that in order to be a complete or felicitous bribe, at least three of the four phases must be completed. That is, there must be a problem statement, a proposal, and a completion. The extension phase, though quite common to bribe events, is not required for felicity.

An example of a successful and complete bribe event took place in the well-known Brilab investigation (Brilab stands for Bribery of Labor Unions) carried out by the FBI. The target was primarily union labor leaders in the Southwest. To ensure authenticity, the FBI used a cooperating witness, Joe Hauser, to talk with labor leaders under the disguise of an insurance executive. Hauser would ask labor leaders to open up their medical insurance plans for renegotiation and bidding in return for a cut of the ensuing profit. Selections from an actual tape recording in that investigation illustrate how the bribe event structure is completed in an actual bribe (table 2.2).

Did Senator Williams accept a bribe?

Having discovered what the structure of a completed and felicitous bribe event actually looks like, we can then compare other

Table 2.2 Bribe event structure shown in actual bribe event

Phase	Joe Hauser	Target
Problem	We'd like to get some state business.	I will have to work out something, Joe, where you could visit with the trustees.
	Do you control Mr Gordon?	He'll go along with a lot of the things I recommend.
	How do you and I develop a relationship?	I have a public relations firm ... and I do business other than what I'm doing here.
Proposal	I can give you $2,000 now, with a 50–50 split of the commission.	Keep talking.
	I deal only with you. There's $4,000 a month possible in this.	We'll deal on a case by case basis. Can you handle X Insurance Company politics?
Completion	Here's $2,000. Let's shake hands on it. Do we have a deal?	We have a deal.
Extension		There's 50 people I can send you. I have contacts in Boston.

alleged bribe offers and acceptances to this model in order to determine whether or not bribery actually took place. Such a comparison can enable us to distinguish the *appearance* of bribery from an actual event.

The case of Senator Harrison A. Williams Jr, who was convicted of bribery in the FBI's Abscam (short for Arab scam) operation, is a case in point. Over a period of some 15 months, beginning in 1978, several scenarios were constructed by the FBI to capture Senator Williams on tape in an illegal act, committing a language crime. Williams had attracted the interest of the agents when it became clear that he was interested in assisting his long-time friend and attorney, Alexander Feinberg, to get a loan for a potential business venture involving the purchase of a defunct titanium mine in Virginia. Although it is clear from the taped conversations that the product of that mine would be the type of titanium used in producing paint, the government consistently inferred that the intent of the venture was to sell a metal titanium product to government contractors for use as a coating on super-sonic or space vehicles.

In this scam operation, the FBI enlisted the help of a very successful con-man, Mel Weinberg, who was paid $2,000 a month by the government for his expertise. In most instances, Weinberg was assisted by an agent, Anthony Amoroso, who went by the alias of Tony DeVito. These men posed as representatives of Abdul Enterprises, a foreign-owned business that represented a sheik allegedly from the United Arab Emirates. Cooperating with the FBI, the Chase Manhattan Bank agreed to represent to anyone who might wish to check on Abdul Enterprises, that it indeed had an account containing millions of dollars in that bank. The front, then, appeared to be legitimate. In fact, just before Williams's trial began, US District Court Judge John Fullam went out of his way to criticize the government's treatment of Williams, noting that the senator was doing nothing more than seeking finance for a legitimate business deal.

On November 27, 1979, a high-level FBI memorandum revealed that after 13 months of pursuit of the senator, the Abscam prosecutors admitted that they had no real case against him. This FBI memo, which was withheld from the senator and his attorneys during his trial by US District Court Judge George Pratt, said: "It would be necessary to recontact Williams to obtain an overt action on his part ... Attempts should be made to elicit from Senator Williams whether or not he wanted his shares (in the titanium mine) hidden." The memo continued that such information needed to be obtained in order "to prove that Senator Williams" had broken the law.

It is not necessary to see this memo to determine that the government did not have the proof they needed at this time. The tapes themselves clearly reveal that the memo writer was accurate. A tape on October 7, 1979, contained the following exchange:

Weinberg: Sandy spoke about you going to declare 17 million dollars profit or something.

Williams: No, I'm going to find a way to protect myself with some kind of *declaration*. I'm going to have to *go public* with something or other. We haven't figured that out.

DeVito: The original thing was that your shares were in Alex' name ... everything was going to be *hidden* ... our end had to be *hidden* too. In other words, they were buying it because of the position that you were going to have in the thing ... Everybody can declare. *You can't*. They are not going to buy the premise that you're going to declare. If you were going to declare we'd have to go back and reform the corporation.

Williams: Uh-huh. Well, this is where the lawyer comes in Alex. We can *blind trust* me, you know. That's up to the law department.

The importance of this passage is as follows. Weinberg had introduced the topic of the senator's statement that he would declare his interest. Senator Williams responds that he meant that he needed to find a way to protect himself but that it would have to be public, some kind of declaration. At this point, DeVito comes in to reinforce Weinberg by reminding the senator of the "original thing."

To DeVito's last utterance, about the Arabs not buying it on the premise that the senator would declare, Senator Williams offers an "I hear you" lax-token response (*uh-huh*) and then defers his response: "Well, this is where the lawyer comes in Alex." This response is consistent with the senator's many "see Alex" deferring responses throughout these conversations. It can in no way be treated as affirmation. Quite the contrary, the senator is saying that the way to do it has not yet been worked out: "That's up to the law department."

Later, in the same October 7 conversation, Williams continues his insistence that any interest he might have in the proposed business must be worked out legally:

> *DeVito*: George got upset . . . says how can the senator declare. It'll be known. My understanding of it was you were gonna declare it, but *in some other way*.
>
> *Williams*: That's exactly . . . you hit it, right. There are ways to be on a certain record. Now if it's a *blind trust*, that's the way for my purposes.

Again, later in that conversation, DeVito says that the senator "was coming up with some kind of a *gimmick*." To this, Williams responds, "Well, there we have it under the *trust*."

Throughout several conversations the tension is between the terms used by Weinberg and DeVito, "hidden interest," "secret," "gimmick," "some other way," and the terms used by Williams and his attorney, Alex Feinberg, "blind trust," "go public," "declare it." By November 27, the government assessed what they had and concluded what is obvious from the tapes, that it was the government suggesting any illegality, not the senator, and that Williams and Feinberg were guilty of no more than declaring that any potential involvement of the senator would have to be done legally and above board. This scenario clearly had failed so a new one had to be created.

In their new scenario for Williams, the FBI resorted to the most drastic measure in all the Abscam operation, the use of a fake sheik. On January 15, 1980, agent Richard Farhart donned the robes of an Arab and practiced a foreign accent in order to meet with the senator in a room at the Plaza Hotel in New York City. Immediately preceding this meeting, however, was the famous "coaching" conversation, in which Weinberg and Angelo Errichetti, Mayor of Camden who was an already co-opted conspirator, urged and coached Williams in what to say to the sheik. They produced a list of 28 different statements to impress this foreigner, including "your influence to get contracts," "how important you are," "you are the deal," etc. Williams, amused at their arrogance and in disagreement with their coaching, is then introduced to the sheik by agent DeVito.

It is interesting and informative to note that during this meeting with the sheik, Senator Williams produces none of the coaching directives, a fact missed by most listeners to the tape, including Williams's fellow senators. In fact, during Williams's Senate Ethics Committee hearings, Senator Mark O. Hatfield, Republican of Oregon, a man known for his perception and compassion, came up to Williams during a break and said, "Pete, I just don't see how you could blow your own horn that way." Senator Hatfield, like all the others, had completely missed the point. It was Errichetti and DeVito who uttered these words, not Senator Williams. Hatfield, like his fellow senators and like the jury who convicted Williams, was contaminated by context and could not keep clearly in mind exactly who said what. The appearance of illegality had taken precedence over the facts, the same problem most juries have with tape cases.

It was during his meeting with agent Farhart, acting as the sheik, that the FBI's final scenario with Senator Williams occurs. Farhart talks about the titanium mine he is expected to finance with his loan, then haltingly introduces the topic of the possibility of the senator introducing legislation that would lead to the sheik's establishing permanent residence in the United States. This was the quid in the quid pro quo used by the FBI in all its Abscam cases. Specifically, the congressmen were asked to introduce this special legislation and, in return, the sheik would give them $25,000, $50,000 or some amount of cash. This scheme had already netted Congressmen Ozzie Meyers and Richard Kelly, among others and it seemed to be worth another try with Senator Williams.

In the Williams case, then, both the quid, the agreement to introduce such legislation, and the quo, the acceptance of bribe money, must be clearly evident, just as it was with the others caught in this scam. As we shall see, neither of these definitions was achieved by the FBI with Senator Williams. First, let us look at the actual words used by both the sheik and the senator to see if any agreement to introduce legislation is achieved.

To Farhart's question about whether or not this request for legislation is "a problem," the senator says that such legislation *can* be accomplished although not easily. The senator's exact words were:

- It's not easy
- there have to be good reasons
- it meets some criteria
- it's harder now than it was five years ago
- it has been restricted
- best results when a person of good character is here
- if the person were made to return to his country he would face great personal hardship
- the situation has to be fully understood
- there are criteria
- it's an exceptional situation
- after full knowledge of your situation
- it is processed through a committee
- then also in the other body (of Congress)
- Quite frankly I can't issue that
- I cannot personally
- it goes through the whole dignified process of passing a law

In terms of the sheik's request for legislation, the senator promised no positive results. His predictions were guarded, if not negative, saying only that he would help the sheik do the things that would bring the sheik's case to consideration through proper channels. To guard against the words "doing the things" being possibly misunderstood as covert or suspicious, the senator modeled what he meant. He asked the sheik for background information, references, and facts as a means of building his dossier if such a process were even to begin. There are those, including prosecutor Thomas Puccio, who believe that Williams, in agreeing to help the sheik even in this way, was agreeing to sponsor legislation for the sheik's immigration. Careful listening, however, clearly shows that Williams was simply laying out the map of how this very difficult task might be done, should the facts of the case merit it. There is no blatant agreement to do it; only a realistic statement about how such legislation has to be accomplished. Thus, the government's effort to establish a quid pro quo which was, essentially, sponsor legislation for the offer of a loan for the titanium mine project, utterly fails.

This failure must also have been clear to agent Farhart, who then turns his attention to any possible influence peddling the senator may have done:

Farhart:	Uh, since, uh, last we spoke of the, uh, uh, the tita-nium, uh, any problems? Has any progress towards, uh, we said several people you would contact, regarding . . .
Williams:	I haven't.

Here, as elsewhere in these tapes, two meanings of "people to contact" are present. The government version is "influence peddling with government agencies or contractors." But, once again, careful examination of all earlier tapes (there were 58 in all, but only seven in which Senator Williams is present) clearly demonstrates that all statements about "government contracts" are uttered either outside Williams's presence or, on two instances in a June 28, 1979 video tape, one by agent DeVito and the other by Angelo Errichetti:

DeVito:	And he feels that with you behind this thing, with the people you know, the ah government contracts, available, you know, this whole – thing –
Williams:	Right through.
DeVito:	– is that you can move all these things . . .

On the surface, it might appear that Senator Williams agrees that he can move things through, namely government contracts. But careful analysis of this exchange does not support this misperception of what is said.

First, it must be noted that a video constraint makes this passage less clear than it might be. Several exchanges earlier, the camera focus-framing moved from Senator Williams and Errichetti to the sheik and DeVito. During the exchange cited above, we can see only DeVito and the sheik. It is disputable, for one thing, whether or not it was Senator Williams or Errichetti who said "Right through." Their voices are both deep and it had been Errichetti who had made the three previous statements and who made the following three as well.

But even under this difficult constraint, let us examine DeVito's proposition. He introduced it as "the people that you know," indicating a focus on contacts, the major subject of the preceding coaching session. With such a topic focus, it is quite likely that "government contracts" could be understood by the senator as "government contacts." The "r" sound in English is one of the most difficult to perceive. It is one of the last sounds learned by children, one of the hardest to learn by foreigners and the one sound which has widest dialectal variation in English. DeVito's Eastern dialect is a relatively r-less dialect to begin with and his weak pronunciation of that sound, coupled with the topic focus of "the people you know" makes this word a candidate for confusion here.

The senator's response, "Right through," is equally interesting here. Although the surface understanding of its meaning might be thought to be "moving the contracts right through" it is of greatest importance to note that DeVito's sentence, before the senator interrupted with "Right through" has not yet produced a main verb. The verb, *move*, is spoken by DeVito *after* the senator's words so that there is no way that the senator could have understood DeVito's meaning of "moving contracts through" until he had heard the main verb which follows.

What, then, did Senator Williams mean by his "Right through?" Since the topic focus of this incomplete sentence was on people he knew, leading to a likely ascribed hearing of "contracts" as "contacts," the senator's "Right through" most likely refers to people, from those he knows right through government contacts. Earlier talk about contacts with the senator had focused on contacts with paint company officials who may be able to use the eventual titanium product and not with government officials who recognize the need for the sort of titanium used for space products, a type which was quite different from the kind their hoped-for mine might produce. The senator agrees, in these earlier tapes, to the fact that government officials need titanium but *not* to the need to talk to them about their future product, since it is irrelevant to their needs. Therefore, when DeVito says either "government contracts" or "government contacts," in the passage quoted above, it is not the first time the senator has heard this odd statement, even if Williams perceives DeVito to be saying "contract" rather than "contacts." There is no hope for government contracts for paint-producing titanium, even if the senator had agreed to try.

In any case, to Farhart on January 15, Williams responds that he has *not* talked to people, whatever "people" may have meant to the agent/sheik. At this point, no doubt disappointed once again by Williams's response, Farhart goes for the home-run, the offer of a cash bribe, as follows:

Farhart: I will, for your help, uh, assistance, I would like to
              give you . . . some money for, for permanent residence.
Williams: No. No. No. No, when I work in that kind of activity,
              it is purely a public, not uh, No, within my position,
              when I deal with law and legislation, it's not within
              . . . (*telephone rings, interrupting*). My only interest is
              to see this come together.
(*DeVito then enters the room and tells the sheik to take the call
in another room.*)

When the sheik comes back to the room, Senator Williams
carefully explains his role in all this, by way of explaining to a
foreigner, with perhaps different values or ethical norms, why he
could not take money from him:

Williams: No, uh, my interest is with my associates, . . . to see
              this very valuable mining area developed . . . So my
              only interest is to see this come together.

In this instance, a bribe was offered and clearly rejected. Both
the prosecutors and Senate Ethics Committee objected nonetheless, observing that the senator displayed none of the righteous
indignation required of such an offer. In this objection, they display their ignorance of what is at stake when political leaders of
two quite different cultures engage in talk. Of highest importance
is face-saving, dignity and politeness. One simply does not insult
such a person. Even more complex, however, is the possibility
that by uttering such indignation, the sheik could decide to with-
draw the offer of the legitimate loan which was, in Williams's
viewpoint, the sole reason for the meeting anyway. Finally, the
telephone interruption, which was engineered by the government,
effectively blocked our learning whatever the senator might have
planned to say at that time. The call was effectively timed by the
FBI to occur after the bribe was rejected, but before the senator
could elaborate his reasons.

In terms of the previously described structure of a bribe event,
this event was not felicitous but broke down in the proposal
phase (table 2.3).

In light of the senator's clear rejection of the bribe offer, how
could a jury have convicted him of bribery? There are several
reasons, not the least of which was a weak defense by his attorney,
George Koelzer. Clearly, the early scenarios developed by the

Table 2.3 Breakdown of bribe event structure in the Williams case

Phase	Sheik	Williams
Problem	I need legislation	There have to be good reasons
Proposal	I would like to give you some money for permanent residence	No. No. No. No
Completion	None	
Extension	None	

government had failed by their own standards. Even without the FBI internal memorandum of November 29, 1979, there is evidence of their failure. Once a second scenario is attempted, it is clear that the first one is not considered successful, else a second one would not be necessary. The "hidden interest" scenario falls into this category, as did a follow-up scenario in which it was proposed, in Williams's absence, that after the group obtained the loan they would sell the titanium mine and reinvest in other things. There were other scenarios as well, all of which were deemed unincriminating by the FBI itself and from the tape recordings. What then consisted of a bribe?

On August 5, 1979, the senator was on his way to Europe on Senate business, leaving from the John F. Kennedy airport in New York. Before this departure, the FBI had printed a number of stock certificates in the as-yet non-existent corporate entity which planned to get the sheik's loan to begin its existence. Errichetti, DeVito and Weinberg plan to meet Williams at the airport for a brief discussion just before he boards his plane. Abruptly, at the very start of this 12-minute meeting, DeVito hands Williams the stock certificates:

> *DeVito:* I thought that this, uh, you know being you were taking off, that at the appropriate time I wanted to just start off with this to –
> *Errichetti:* We want to make sure that you got them first.
> *Weinberg:* You got them.
> *DeVito:* Here, Give you these . . . These are the certificates and I had Alex endorse them and uh, what's his name, his, uh, the other attorney, uh, witness them so –

Williams: Yeah.
DeVito: Uh –
Williams: Very good, okay, Tony. Yeah. Uh-huh.

Senator Williams is a passive participant in this conversation, responding with "uh-huh," "okay," and "yeah" to 36 of the 38 statements initiated by DeVito and Weinberg.

This, in itself, is evidence that the senator was not excited or impressed by receiving these stock certificates unexpectedly. Nor did he in any way indicate that he believed anything would ever become of the proposed business venture. Further evidence of his lack of concern for these certificates is the fact that he neither acknowledged receipt of them nor thanked Weinberg and DeVito for them. They were, in his mind, unexpected, rather fanciful, if not untimely, symbols of an unreal hope. Later evidence of any value Williams may have placed on the stocks can be seen by the fact that they remained in his airplane carry-on bag for months after Williams returned from Europe. This bag sat open, on the floor of his Senate office, readily available to anyone who might think them valuable enough to steal.

At trial, however, the prosecution made much of these stock certificates. In fact, the government considered Williams's acceptance of these pieces of paper related to a non-existent company as the quo of the quid pro quo. Their claim was that the senator had agreed to sponsor legislation for the sheik's immigration (the quid) in return for the worthless shares in a non-existing company. As we have noted, the government was clearly overreaching on the *quid* part – Williams agreed only to help this foreign dignitary get his dossier together for possible application. The government utterly failed in their best shot for the *quo* part, when Williams rejected the cash bribe four months after the JFK airport stock certificate caper.

Now, at the time of the trial, the prosecution needed to rebuild the stocks scenario as the *quo*, even though the FBI internal memorandum of November 29 had indicated its incriminating power. The first step by the prosecution was to keep this memorandum from the defense. During the standard discovery phase of the pre-trial hearings the government was not obliged to reveal it and made no mention of it. Only through the persistent digging of investigative reporters and attorneys did the memo emerge. By then it was too late. The *appearance* of illegality had overpowered the judgement of the jury, the Senate Ethics Committee and the general public. Senator Williams lost his appeal and went to prison for bribery, even though both the *quid* and the *quo* were absent.

Did John McNown and John Poli accept a bribe?

Not all bribery cases are as celebrated as Abscam and not all suspects are well-known politicians. The "little guys" also can get embroiled in the activities of the FBI or other government agencies to capture them on tape saying things that may later be thought to be illegal.

John McNown and John Poli were two such little guys. As two middle-aged farmers in Nevada, their lives were centered on growing avocados until asked, one day, to serve on the brothel commission of a Nevada county that had legalized prostitution. "Somebody has to do it," they figured, so they accepted the offer. In the process of serving on this commission, their lives became dramatically changed. They had to deal with a type of person they had not dealt with before and, as we shall see, they were totally unprepared for it.

Part of their responsibility, as commissioners, was to screen applicants for brothel licenses. One day a woman from San Francisco approached them for a license and their suspicions were raised. To them, she seemed like a representative of the San Francisco Mafia. They discussed this after she left and devised a plan to test out their doubts. If she were really a Mafia representative, they reasoned, she would respond positively to their suggestion that she pay them extra money on the side to help get the license. This plan was, at best, stupid but only small portions of life get carried out with intelligence by most people. And these commissioners were not immune to the human failures of logic.

Janice, whom McNown and Poli believed to be a madam, went straight to the FBI and reported that she was being extorted. The FBI wired her with a Nagra recording device and sent her to a follow-up meeting at Howard's Lounge. There, in a rather small eating area amidst other diners, the three of them sat at a small square table, with Janice seated between the men.

Table 2.4   Thematic distribution of topics among Janice, Poli and McNown

Theme	Janice	Poli	McNown
Money	14	0	0
Car/driving	0	2	2
Trailer permit	2	4	1
Small talk	8	4	6

The tape-recorded conversation reveals 43 topics during this 27-minute talk. Janice introduced 24 of the topics, over half of them. Poli introduced ten topics and McNown nine. What is of most interest, however, is the thematic distribution of the topics introduced by all three, as shown in table 2.4.

The first thing that is striking as one hears the conversation is that all money topics are introduced by Janice and none are introduced by Poli and McNown. This is particularly odd since the two men are presumably extorting Janice for $50,000. It is unusual for extortionists not to bring up the subject. They do bring up the subject of the trailers that now exist for the purpose of legalized prostitution, they ask whether or not Janice would like to buy such trailers and they discuss the possibility of going for a ride together in their car.

It is Janice's money topics, however, which carry the burden of the conversation. She reports that $50,000 is too much money, requests a more reasonable figure and finally offers $35,000 with $5,000 right now. The responses of Poli and McNown to the money topics are non-committal, mumblingly incoherent grunts until Janice mentions that she has $5,000 with her *right now*. At this point, Poli and McNown become animated, speaking rapidly at the same time. Obviously, their rather stupid plan to see whether or not Janice is Mafia-based had taken an unpredicted direction. She actually had the money with her and she actually intended to give it to them. Their response to this point would be crucial. They could either take the money and enter the world of crime that they had hitherto avoided or they could say no and look very foolish for having suggested money in the first place.

Since the event was tape recorded, it should have been a simple matter to note what they said and to base both the prosecution and the defense on these words. But things are never that simple. The tape recording was not of a high quality. The setting was a noisy restaurant with dishes banging, music playing and the voices of other customers and waitresses throughout. To make matters even worse, Poli and McNown suddenly experienced heightened emotion, clipping their words, talking over each other and speaking very rapidly. The prosecution and the defense disagreed totally on the transcript of what Poli said to Janice's offer of $35,000 with $5,000 right now. The prosecution transcript read:

Poli: No, I would take a bribe, wouldn't you?

The defense transcript, in sharp contrast, read:

Poli: No, I wouldn't take a bribe, would you?

There were many other differences between the government's and the defense's transcripts; this one, however, was the most crucial. On the witness stand, I pointed out that I had played the tape over and over again, some 50 times, before deciding on the defense version. My decision was based on two important factors besides the audible sounds themselves.

For one thing, there were indisputably nine syllables uttered here. Both the government and defense transcripts agree on this. But the speech rhythms that separate the nine syllables from each other are quite different in the two transcripts, as follows (– indicates a syllable):

Government transcript:
Poli: _____, __ _____ ____ __ _____, ____ ____ ____?
          No, I would take a bribe, wouldn't you

Defense transcript:
Poli: _____, __ _____ ____ _____ __ _____, ____ ____?
          No, I wouldn't take a bribe, would you

That is, the government showed a syllable division between pause junctures of 1 – 5 – 3; the defense showed a syllable division between the pause junctures of 1 – 6 – 2. The key words were *would* and *wouldn't*, one syllable and two syllables, respectively.

The answer to the problem is found in the speech itself. Where did the syllable junctures fall? I played this portion of the tape to the jury and had them "beat out" the syllables, much as a child would do in beginning reading class. The answer then became clear: Poli was saying:

Poli: No, I would n't take a bribe, would you?

The second factor that argued for the defense transcript is found in the first word of the utterance, *No*. It is rare, if not totally impossible to follow a negative introducer, "No," with a positive statement, "I would take a bribe." There is a grammatical harmony in English which attracts negative to negative. Thus, "No, I wouldn't" is far more likely than "No, I would."

In any case, these words were followed by Poli's: "I wouldn't take it today; I would wait." Once again, these words were not the most clever thing Poli could have said. He did not agree to take a bribe, to be sure, but he did not disagree either. He only deferred the decision. Seconds later, they decide to leave. Poli, nearest to the door, gets up and leaves first. As Janice stands up, she slips $5,000 cash on the chair of McNown as he is half-standing. She says: "Just take it. Here." McNown, still half-up and half-down, looks at his chair with the money on it and asks "What do you mean?" Janice zips her purse, says "I'm gonna take off" and rushes to the lady's room where she is being monitored by the FBI.

McNown is now left standing at the table with $5,000 cash on his chair. Poli has already paid the check and is outside. What should McNown do with the money? He shrugs his shoulders, picks it up and joins Poli in the car. As they drive away, Poli breathes a sigh of relief and says "Well, I'm sure glad we didn't take that money!" McNown looks at him and says, "What do you mean, we didn't take that money?" Poli stops the car at once, turns around and drives directly back to Howard's Lounge. As they get out of their car they are arrested, handcuffed and taken to jail.

Our original question, and the question for the jury to decide, is: "Did Poli and McNown accept a bribe?" There can be no question about whether or not Janice offered a bribe. Clearly, she did. But to *accept* something implies two things:

1 Receipt of something.
2 Agreement or consent to receive it.

One might argue that Poli and McNown received the money. It is quite another matter to claim that they agreed to receive it. For example, a baseball may come crashing through my living room window and land on my floor. Clearly, I have received the baseball but I most certainly did not agree to receive it. It would be difficult, indeed, to prove that I had accepted the baseball.

There were, in this conversation, many evidences that Poli and McNown were not in agreement with receiving the money. We have already mentioned their statement that they would not take a bribe. The government, of course, disputed this statement. But there is other evidence of their lack of agreement as well. We mentioned the money topic earlier. Now let us examine this topic more closely. First of all, recall that Janice introduced this topic each of the 14 times it came up. The responses of Poli and McNown to these 14 topic introductions is the key to whether or not they were agreeable to accept the bribe. One might expect a person who is agreeable to say "yes, yes, give me the money," as Congressman Ozzie Myers indicated in Abscam. Anything short of such agreement casts doubt on the speaker's willingness, eagerness, and consent to accept it. These 14 money topic introductions can be summarized as follows:

Janice	*Poli/McNown*
16 I need something more reasonable.	(Change subject to car)
18 How about in two to six months?	Put it in a trust.
19 $50,000 is high.	Could you put that in writing?
20 Is there anyone else I should pay?	There isn't anyone.
24 Do I pay something each year?	No.
25 $50,000 is high.	(No response)
26 The price is high. I want to cooperate.	You won't be the first one to try that.
27 I want to come in right.	What's "right?"

29 Will you come down?	(Explains why they came up with that figure)
31 How about $35,000, with $5,000 right now?	No, I wouldn't take a bribe, would you?
32 You want to wait?	I would wait.
34 How about $30,000?	(No response)
37 There'd better not be any extras.	We'll come by and see you once in awhile.
41 Just take it. Here!	What do you mean?

Any analysis of these 14 responses by Poli and McNown must be, as always, set in the context in which they occurred. Keep in mind that these two men went into the meeting with the express purpose of determining whether or not Janice represented the Mafia. They had suggested that she give them money in a previous, unrecorded meeting. Now they are meeting her and her reaction to their suggestion would be critical to them. With such a schema, there is no need to be cautious about money topics, for this is exactly what they expected her to talk about, particularly if she was sent by the Mafia. By the same token, there was also no need for these two men to reject the offer, since, to them at least, neither accepting nor rejecting it was the issue. The issue was whether or not she would offer it.

The surprise in all this for Poli and McNown was that Janice offered them cash on the spot. To this point, the game had been played in the abstract and hypothetical. They wanted to find out if she *would* offer money for the license. They could defer her offer as long as it was hypothetical ("put it in a trust" and "put it in writing"), but once the money was flashed, the hypothetical was transformed into serious reality.

Having said that they would not take a bribe and that they would wait, the conversation comes to a close. In their own minds, Poli and McNown could leave now unscathed. They undoubtedly thought that Janice was indeed Mafia based, for she had expressed willingness to give them money. In that sense, their stupid plan had worked. Poli bolts for the door but McNown is caught behind Janice. Never before had he faced such a problem. Should he leave the cash on the chair? Should he chase Janice to the lady's room and force her to take it back? Should he pick it up until he could figure out what to do with it? It is difficult to know what *we* might have done under such circumstances. McNown made the wrong decision, as hindsight made so clear. But it was a decision that any less than brilliant person might have made under the pressure he felt at the time.

None of the 14 responses displays a greedy desire for cash. Several merely defer a decision. At least one says "no, I won't do it." Realizing the potential ambiguity of the men's position, the prosecution came down very hard on their interpretation of the crucial nine syllables. If they would convince the jury that Poli was actually saying that they *would* take a bribe, their carrying off the $5,000 might be explained.

The first trial ended in a hung jury. Some believed the prosecutor. Some believed the defense. The judge allowed both transcripts when, after listening to the tape, he could not in his own mind decide which way was accurate. When the case was retried some months later, the prosecution changed its transcript extensively. Now it matched the defense transcript of the first trial in every respect except, of course, the crucial nine syllable utterance. In the retrial, the judge would not permit my testimony.

But had they agreed to take the bribe? Not according to the words that were on the tape. They had acted stupidly to position themselves in the meeting at Howard's Lounge in the first place. But they had not accepted the money. Like the baseball crashing into my window, they *received* the money. But they had not accepted it. They made direct statements that they would not accept it. They made no statements that they would accept it. Their responses to Janice's 14 money topics indicated no desire to accept it. Finally, when McNown told Poli that he indeed *had* the money, Poli turned the car around and drove directly back to the restaurant to give it back. None of this sounds very much like two extortionists greedy for bribe money. But it must have sounded that way to the jury in the retrial, especially since that jury was prohibited from the sort of assistance about conversational structure that might have helped them understand what they heard.

Life on the edge of legality is a teetering rock. Of course, a person is stupid to get out on that rock in the first place. But stupidity is not illegal. It just looks that way to many. Little guys can be as stupid as politicians or corporate executives. When they are, they fall off the teetering rocks. Poli and McNown should never have played detective in the first place, perhaps. At least not that way. But even with all the coloration of guilt manufactured by the prosecutor, they never "accepted" the bribe; they just received it. And the beats and pauses of their speech indicate clearly that they did not agree to take a bribe. In fact, they disagreed. Nonetheless they proved that little guys can be indicted too. Both Poli and McNown were convicted in their retrial. Other things may have supported their conviction for all I know, but if the tape was the primary evidence the defense interpretation was as plausible as the prosecution's.

3

Offering Bribes

In the case of Senator Williams and again in the case of Poli and McNown, the bribery issue hinged strongly on whether or not there was an acceptance of anything that might be considered a bribe. In both cases, something was received. Williams *received* some pieces of paper that even the government did not think were worth anything. Poli and McNown *received* $5,000 cash under the most tainted of circumstances, when Janice left it on McNown's chair. Bribery cases must be carefully examined not only for whether or not something was *received* but also for whether or not a bribe was actually ever *offered*.

It might seem that nothing could be more obvious than whether or not a person is actually offering a bribe. But this is simply not the case. I recently presented a list of sentences to a group of teachers and asked them to identify the speech acts (requests, reporting facts, opinions, denials, promises, offers, etc.) which these sentences represented. The sentence "I'll give you $5 if you'll wash my car" was regularly identified as a "bribe". To the average person, the difference between an offer and a bribe may not be all that clear. Normal business transactions consist of offers of money or goods for services or goods. We propose a value of one thing for the value of another thing as the basis for an exchange. This is done countless times in any given day. The difference between an offer and a bribe is simply this: in the quid pro quo of a bribe, one of the elements is illegal. What my teachers failed to consider is that there is nothing illegal about the $5 offer of money for the service of washing a car.

As obvious as this may sound, this confusion between offer and bribe is at the very heart of many court cases involving bribery charges. The following three cases illustrate different aspects of this confusion and how they were ultimately resolved by the courts.

Did the agents offer Billy Clayton a bribe?

In their celebrated Brilab investigations in the late seventies, the FBI made use of the con-man, Joe Hauser, to try to convince labor leaders to reopen the bidding on their medical insurance plans so that Hauser's company, the Prudential Insurance Company, could come in with a lower bid and get the business. It should be pointed out that Prudential knew nothing about the FBI's use of their name in this operation. Hauser's approach was to convince the labor leader that the bids should be reopened by offering to split the profits – often amounting to hundreds of thousands of dollars – with the labor leader and by offering a smaller amount of money, between $2,000 and $5,000, up front in good faith.

This operation worked reasonably well for the FBI, and several labor leaders were netted by this approach. Hauser's contact with the head of the operating engineer's union, L. G. Moore, was particularly fruitful, leading him to several other targets. When Moore reported that he was personally acquainted with the speaker of the Texas State House of Representatives, Hauser's eyes lit up – here was a golden opportunity to catch a big fish, a politician. Moore made the necessary arrangements and a meeting with Speaker Billy Clayton was arranged at his office on October 19, 1979.

Shortly before this meeting, however, we have several recorded meetings between Hauser and Moore. Though by now co-opted, Moore was, of course, unaware that Hauser was a surrogate government agent. As far as Moore could tell, Hauser was merely a crooked insurance executive. During one of these recorded meetings, however, Hauser urges Moore to take over more of the leadership in their meetings with the contacts that Moore was providing. Hauser knew that his job was to get the FBI operation going well and that his role in it would end when he went to jail and he wanted Moore to extend his work as widely as possible. In typical Texas metaphor, Hauser urges Moore to take over as "quarterback" in their meeting with Clayton.

At the very beginning of their meeting with Clayton, this leadership role is introduced:

Moore: Well let me ask you something.

Hauser: Let's, let's get into that. Why don't we get into that right now?

Moore: Can I, can I do it Joe? And I wanna, we wanna, we want to, and if it puts you in a bad situation you tell me. We want to make a contribution to your campaign. If that creates a problem for us under this type of circumstances, we don't want to do it.

It is clear from Moore's speech that his role is somewhat confusing even to himself. Moore starts by asking, "let *me* ask you something." Hauser interrupts and says "*Let's* get into that. Why don't *we* get into that?" Moore takes the cue. He had been speaking of *me* to this point. Hauser is suggesting *we*. Moore sees the chance to try out his leadership role and asks Joe's permission "Can I, can I do it Joe?" Apparently receiving silent consent, Moore launches out as quarterback for the first time: "And *I* wanna ..." Moore pauses and realizes his pronoun problem. "This is a *we* operation, not an *I* operation," Moore thinks to himself. Immediately, Moore self-corrects his pronoun to *we*: "We wanna, *we* want to ... *we* want to make a contribution to your campaign." Throughout this brief, eight-minute conversation, Moore is somewhat confused about which persona he represents. This problem is of the greatest importance because an offer must come from somebody. The question of legality may well hinge on who the offer is from. It is important for the jury to understand the confusion of persona or role representation in order to see how unclear it must have seemed to Speaker Clayton about who was doing the offering and what, if anything, was actually being offered.

And what exactly would this difference be? If it were L. G. Moore personally offering a campaign contribution, there would have been no problem under Texas law. But even this would not be totally clear. When a person says "I," there are several meanings: *I* personally and individually, *I* as representative of an organization, *I* as the agent of some other relationship which is inferred or explicit, etc. For example, when a boss says, "I fire you," the boss uses *I* to mean, "In my role as boss," not *I* personally. But when a person says "*We* would like to give you a campaign contribution," the *we* can mean any of the following:

1　*We*, as the organization I represent.
2　The other person here with me now plus myself.
3　The two organizations represented by myself and the other person here with me.
4　Myself and other persons not here with me at present.
5　Myself, the other person here with me plus other unspecified persons who are not here with us at present

The question of Clayton's perception of what Moore was saying, then, hinges on how he inferred the meaning of Moore's use of *we*. If the campaign contribution is from Moore alone, the contribution is perfectly legitimate and clear. If it is from Moore and Hauser or their organizations, it is unclear exactly where it is coming from. If one of the components of *we* is the Prudential Insurance Company, and if it is given during the same meeting in which Clayton might be seen to be helping Prudential reopen the bids, then the contribution could be seriously questioned.

Some bribery cases hinge on whether or not agreements are made. Others hinge on vague uses of words. In this case, by far the most crucial language issue is the use of pronouns. It is now instructive to examine all of the proposals made in this conversation, including the one just discussed. There were five different proposals made in this passage of the conversation. The five proposals concerned three topics: saving the State some money, the campaign contribution, and, finally, Hauser's offer to split the sales commission with Clayton. Table 3.1 outlines these proposals and displays Billy Clayton's responses to them.

First Hauser proposes that if the insurance bids could be reopened, the State could save a million dollars. Clayton agrees that this is good and agrees to help reopen the bids, following acceptable procedures. Moore follows with an offer of a campaign contribution from an unspecified *we*. Clayton defers this offer saying, "Let's take care of this thing first (the first proposal, to save the state a million), *then* let's think about a contribution." Undaunted by the deferral, L. G. Moore then changes pronouns and asks if he personally ("I, L. G. Moore," appositionally clarified) could make such a contribution. Clayton agrees. (This is, by the way, perfectly legal.) At this point, L. G. Moore turns to Hauser and says, "Give me the deal." Hauser's voice then counts out, "one, two, three, four, five," and places it on Clayton's desk. Later, when Moore retells these events to the undercover FBI agents, he points out that Hauser handed him $5,000 from his pocket. While the money is on Clayton's desk, Moore then redefines Clayton's agreement to accept Moore's personal contribution by changing his pronoun to *we* and by upping the ante in amount. Clayton's response was *not* to Moore's proposal with the upped-ante, but to Hauser's first proposal, to save the State money. Analysts of conversation have long recognized Clayton's strategy here as a redirect to a topic more appropriate to the conversation. Speaker Clayton's response was about the announced or official purpose of the conversation. It is also likely that he was quite aware of the non-verbal event which had just taken place. After Moore offered a personal contribution, he turned and got the money from Hauser.

This physical event could well have defined for Clayton the reference to *we* in this proposal enough, at least, to cause him to become very cautious and to try to divert the topic back to the appropriate one. Moore responded to Clayton's response with "That's all the commitment we want out of you." Hauser added, "Okay, that's all we want." Clayton then verified the meaning of his response with "I think that's what part of my job is, to try to save the State."

Hauser then quickly relieves Moore as quarterback, and with very specific language indicates that there would be a saving of 1.2 million and that he intends to keep half and give the other half to Clayton. Speaker Clayton clearly rejects this proposal and once again returns to the official, announced topic of saving the State a million dollars. Clayton recycles the topic of saving the State money four times during this part of the conversation.

The question for the jury here, of course, is whether or not Billy Clayton was actually ever offered a bribe. Five proposals were made by Hauser and Moore. It is clear that Clayton is responsive to the proposal of saving the State over a million dollars. What politician would not be? To the second proposal, "*we* want to make a campaign contribution," Clayton senses trouble with the *we* and tries to defer the topic until after the

Table 3.1 Billy Clayton's responses to Hauser and Moore's proposals

| Insurance proposal to save the State money | Hauser and Moore's proposals | | Clayton's responses |
	Campaign contribution	Offer to split commission	
JH: There will be a saving of approximately a million dollars			... anytime you can save the State a buck well by God, I'm for it.
	LGM: We want to make a contribution to your campaign		Let's get this thing and try to take care of it first ... and uh, then, then, then, uh, then let's think about that.
	LGM: Could I, L. G. Moore ... give you a contribution?		Oh, sure.

LGM: We will put, I will, in your whatever you want to run. $100,000 going in and we can prepare to put a half a million

Anytime you can show me where you can save the State money I'll by God, I'll go to battle for you. I think that's what part of my job is ... try to save the State.

LGM: That's all the commitment we want out of you

JH: There's $600,000 every year. I'm keeping 600 and 600 whatever you want to do with it to get the business

... our only position is we don't want to do anything that's illegal or anything to get anybody in trouble and you all don't either.

And this is as legitimate as it can be because anytime somebody can show me how we can help to save the State some money I'm going to bat for it.

insurance proposal is discussed. Noting Clayton's hesitancy, quarterback Moore redefines the campaign contribution as from him personally. Clayton cannot disagree with this now that it is made specific and legitimate. At this point, Clayton has been offered a campaign contribution and he has at least tentatively agreed to accept it.

Now Moore switches back to *we* again, but even now he is confused: "We will put, I will, in your whatever. . . ." At this point, Moore gets $5,000 from Hauser and puts it on Clayton's desk. Moore then ups the ante to $100,000 and up to half a million. Clayton senses trouble and shifts the topic back to the reason for their being there in the first place, the insurance contract. Hauser senses that they are losing it at that point and ups the ante to $600,000 and, for the first time, suggests the illegality of what they are doing: "I'm keeping 600 and 600 whatever you want to do with it to get the business." Here, at last, is the quid pro quo and the suggestion of illegality. But it occurs *after* the money clearly designated as a campaign contribution has been offered and received.

Clayton's response to this is crucial. If he were to smile, turn his head or agree to the illegality in any way, the FBI would have their pigeon. But he doesn't do this. He says: "Our only position is we don't want to do anything that's illegal or anything to get anybody in trouble and you all don't either." He just wants to save the State some money.

Clayton was not offered a bribe. He was offered a campaign contribution. After the contribution was delivered to his desk, the suggestion that it was a bribe was made. But history can't be rewritten in this way. We can't reclassify an act after it has been uttered. This was the essential issue for the jury to consider. Had Clayton agreed to Hauser's rewriting of history, he would have gone to jail. He did not. He clearly disagreed with it in a wonderfully exculpatory statement.

A bribe offer can only be made on a quid pro quo that has not yet occurred. Once a legitimate offer has occurred and has been accepted, it cannot be reclassified as a quid pro quo bribe offer without the agreement of the person to whom it was offered. Hauser's bribe offer, therefore, never occurred as a bribe offer. It was roughly equivalent to his saying something like the following:

We just gave you money that we called a campaign contribution.
It really wasn't a campaign contribution, even though that's what
we said it was. You accepted it then so now you have to realize
that it was really a bribe. We didn't mean what we said before.

Such reasoning does not work. With careful teaching about such
things, the jury came to the same conclusion and Clayton was
acquitted.

Did the agents offer Henry Ingram a bribe?

As we noted earlier, little guys get caught the same way that
politicians do. Billy Clayton was a big fish, a capstone to the
Brilab operation in the same way that Senator Williams was the
capstone to the Abscam plan. We have noted that the bribe offer
was never really made to Clayton. A similar situation happened
to the Sheriff of Jasper County, South Carolina, Clifford Brantley
and a Hilton Head real estate agent, Henry Ingram.

It is difficult to know exactly why the FBI initiated their operation in South Carolina, but in the spring of 1983 they decided
to enter Jasper County and set up a gambling operation. During
the month of May, FBI 302 reports exist concerning meetings
with Ingram and Brantley but, as is often the case in such operations, no tape recordings were made. This is one of the clear
weaknesses in the FBI's procedure, one which is common to most
tape cases. Whatever the agent chooses to write down is the only
record of that event and often the predicate for the following
taping is layed without any possible manner of verification.

The four FBI 302 reports of May 1983, all written by special
agent Theodore J. Domine Jr, make claims that the defendants
later vehemently denied. Domine claimed, for example, that Ingram
advised him that he provided gambling chips for payoffs on poker
machines, that Ingram would introduce Domine to Sheriff Brantley
so that Domine could payoff Brantley for protection, that Ingram
requested $200 to give Brantley as a payoff, along with other
illegal statements. No tape recording exists to support these claims
and Ingram states, in sharp contrast, that he met Domine only to
show him various buildings that were for rent and to advise him

that if he intended to use a building for private gambling parties he should check with the sheriff to see to it that he was complying with the law in all matters. The way the FBI works in this, however, is unverifiable. The FBI claims, as a result of these 302 reports, that an adequate predicate existed to investigate Brantley and Ingram more thoroughly. Which is exactly what they did.

The tape recording began on June 23, 1983, when Domine visited Sheriff Brantley in his office. Brantley was known as a kind-hearted, quiet, well-liked, middle-aged black sheriff who had come up the hard way. His civic responsibilities went far beyond that of being sheriff; he was well known as an effective fundraiser for the local senior citizens center. There is no mention of Brantley's senior citizen work in the May 302 reports but three minutes into the conversation Domine hands Brantley $500. Brantley is surprised and says "I want you to know that you are not obligated to me," but accepts the money. Later gifts of $500, $200 and $150 were also allegedly given to Brantley, each time accompanied by the sheriff's statement that it wasn't necessary. Records of the senior citizen center later were seen to have included each of the gifts the agent made to the sheriff. Meanwhile, what Sheriff Brantley told Domine was to get a liquor license, to keep his nose clean, to be decent with his deputies and finally on October 18, 1983:

> Listen, whatever, whatever, whatever you folks give me I already give it to the, I give the senior citizens ... see here, you got to campaign 356 days out of the year ... and that's what I'm doing ... See here, I just wanna give a nice thousand dollar program and then, and, and, and people like you have done made it possible.

Here then, we have the case against Sheriff Brantley: he took some $1,350, according to the FBI, as protection money for the private gambling parties conducted by the FBI. By Brantley's own words and from the files of the senior citizens center, it is clear that the money was all donated to the center for its annual party. To be sure, Brantley could have been clearer about why he accepted the money when it was first given. Perhaps he should not have accepted it at all. But the record was clear enough from the evidence available to the FBI. It was clear that they were not dealing with a hardened criminal; instead, they were facing a civic-minded citizen, rough around the edges perhaps, who seized the opportunity to let a Northern, urban slicker pay for the local charity.

But what about the real estate agent, Henry Ingram? Ingram was a local entrepreneur who had investments in several ventures, including the legal poker machines commonly found in game rooms, drug stores and other places. When Domine came to the area, he found Ingram as a real estate agent who might be able to help him rent or purchase a building in which evening private poker parties could be held.

The topics Ingram introduces in the four tape-recorded conversations in which he appears include advice about whether or not Domine might need a license for private poker parties, how to apply for the license, possible rental properties available, how straight Sheriff Brantley is and criticism of his poker machine competitor Collins. There is, in Ingram's conversation, nothing that even hints at an illegal act. At one point in an early conversation, Domine gives Ingram some money to give to Brantley when he next sees him. Ingram takes the money and later reports that he gave it to the sheriff. There is no indication of what the money is for, nor does Ingram ask.

Analysis of Ingram's speech during the four tape-recorded meetings reveals 99 speech acts. A third of these consists of sales pitches for the rental or purchase of properties Ingram was showing the agent. A further third of the speech acts comprises reports of information about the properties or about various people in the area. The final third of Ingram's speech acts includes requests for information on Domine (where he was from, whether or not he was married, etc.), advice about real estate and local laws and warnings about local customs and people. Ingram does not promise anything, offer anything or accept anything. In short, it is difficult to imagine a more uninteresting conversation from the perspective of illegality. Ingram was indicted largely because he agreed to carry $100 from Domine to Brantley, despite the fact that he did not know what the money was for. This made him, in the eyes of the prosecution, a conspirator. Brantley was indicted for taking money from agent Domine on several occasions, despite the fact that Brantley took it to give to a local charity, and clearly said as much.

Perhaps there is a crime in this case somewhere but it is difficult to imagine why the FBI stretched itself so broadly to find it. The question here, as with Speaker Billy Clayton, is whether or not a bribe was ever offered at all. Certainly, the agent gave money to Ingram to give to the sheriff. Money was certainly received. But was it accepted as a bribe?

And what is the obligation of the person offering the money to be clear and unambiguous about the intent of the offer? Speech act analysis specifies several ways to be clear and avoid ambiguity, as follows:

The performative offer

A performative speech act is one that does the act that it describes by the words it uses. For example, a minister performs the act of marriage by saying "I now pronounce you man and wife." Likewise, a person can be christened with the words, "I hereby do christen you Mary." In order to do such things performatively, one must have the right to do so. Thus, a layman cannot officially unite a couple in marriage. Likewise, the act performed must be possible to perform. If one were to declare, "You are an elephant," these words would most certainly not turn you into an elephant. A performative bribe offer would be one in which no ambiguity of the offer would be possible. Such a statement might be as follows: "I hereby do offer you a bribe for such and such."

Such statements, are, of course, unlikely in a world in which words are more fearful than acts. We shun words like "kill" in favor of "do away with" and "steal" in place of "liberate." People just are not likely to offer a bribe performatively.

The indirect offer

It is much more likely that bribes will be offered indirectly, without using the words of illegality: "If you will do me a little favor, I'll make it up to you real good" is one such approach. The context, of course, makes clear what the "little favor" is and suggests strongly what "make it up to you" means. FBI agents find that they have to resort to indirect bribe offers for fear of frightening off their targets. The difficulty with this approach is obvious, however. A court of law requires specificity, precision of language and the avoidance of ambiguity. Whenever an agent is indirect, he runs serious risks of being misunderstood by the target or, even worse, by the jury who ultimately has to listen to the tape recording. Although indirect bribe offers are more common than performative ones, there is still a certain risk that the target may understand the corrupt intent of the offer and turn it down. This leads to the third, most unclear bribe offer of all.

The embedded offer

The embedded bribe offer lacks both the explicitness of the performative offer and the inferred comprehension of the indirect offer. In the embedded offer, two or more strands of activity occur simultaneously. For example, in the Clayton case the legitimate offer of a campaign contribution is used as a smoke screen for the corrupt suggestion of a bribe. Had Billy Clayton been sufficiently excited about the campaign contribution, he might not have even noticed that the bribe offer statements were being made. Before he knew it, the conversation would be over and he would have failed to reject the bribery overtones and might have given the appearance of guilt. Fortunately for Clayton, he did not get excited about the campaign contribution to this extent, even though it was probably Joe Hauser's fond hope that he would.

In Henry Ingram's case, the embedded offer was so inconspicuous that Ingram never even saw it coming. He was asked to give the sheriff some money on behalf of agent Domine. This seemed innocent enough to Ingram. No mention was made of the money being a bribe. Good Southern hospitality does not permit being too nosey, particularly about money concerns. And, after all, Ingram's job was simply to find a rental property for Domine. His mind was on this topic, as his speech acts clearly indicate.

But the smoke screen worked the way agent Domine wanted it to. Without even knowing that Sheriff Brantley had received over a thousand dollars from Domine, without even knowing that Brantley accepted the money on behalf of the senior citizen's center, Ingram became a part of the alleged bribe offer by simply agreeing to be a messenger for Domine's $100 request. If Domine had performatively told Ingram that the money was a bribe,

Ingram might have had the opportunity to decide whether or not he wished to be a part of an illegal act. Even if Domine had implied that the gift was illegal, Ingram might have had the opportunity to infer illegality and decide his course of action. But when the offer was embedded in vagueness, Ingram never really had a chance. He was caught in the net he had never seen, much less understood.

One might seriously question whether or not an embedded offer of the sort made by agent Domine can actually count as an offer at all. Was the offer of a bribe ever really made? Or did the agent create an illusion?

Did Ken McDonald agree to accept a bribe?

Most people who know the Abscam cases well do not know the Abscam case of Kenneth McDonald. McDonald was a New Jersey business executive, former president of Esterbrook Pen Company, who was, in 1979, vice chairman of the Casino Control Commission of Atlantic City. It was the time of great building activity in Atlantic City, since the State law had been recently changed to permit gambling in that area. The Abscam trial of McDonald never occurred because McDonald died before it reached the court. His family said that he died of a broken heart caused by the shame of being suspected of such complicity. His health was poor to begin with but the family may well have been right.

The various scenario switches of the Abscam operation make its story rather complex to describe, but by the spring of 1979 one scenario involved purchasing casinos with the money to be obtained from the mythical Arab sheik who was seeking asylum in the USA. Angelo Errichetti, the Mayor of Camden, was crucial for this part of the enterprise since he knew the appropriate local people who could help bring this purchase about. Errichetti had already exhibited sufficient evidence of being willing to engage in illegal activity, if necessary, in return for cash. He and Mel Weinberg, the con-man employed by the FBI in the Abscam operation, had joined forces as a rather effective team, although Errichetti was still unaware that Weinberg was working for the government.

On March 5, 1979, Errichetti and FBI agent John McCloud (a pseudonym for special agent John McCarthy) met for dinner with McDonald to discuss the possibility of building a casino. McDonald discusses the history and problems of the new venture into casino building in the State, including the desire to attract conventions, increase the job market, the problem of organized crime moving in, the problem of religious groups opposing casinos, how the Casino Commission works and the current sites and building plans. Then McDonald leaves and Errichetti tells agent McCloud, "I'm hanging my fucking star on this guy. And you know it. Forty, thirty, ten, whatever you say." McCloud responds, "No problem . . . but you can also maybe make a contribution, which you gotta have." Errichetti later says, "Ken's where we have a problem."

The FBI's 302 report of the conversation between McCloud and Errichetti *before* the dinner meeting with McDonald says that McDonald will take $100,000 to handle Abdul Enterprise's casino license application with $10,000 as a down payment. This meeting was not tape recorded, so there is no way to verify that the 302 report was accurate. The dinner meeting *was* tape recorded, however, and the 302 report of that meeting seriously twisted what the tape recording clearly demonstrates. The report by agent McCarthy/McCloud, says: "McDonald then detailed the strength and control of the Casino Control Commission . . . and added that, in effect, the only way to secure a casino license is through cooperation with the Commission." In fact, what McDonald had said was merely a description of how the Commission actually worked.

McCarthy's wording cleverly made this normal and business-like description appear to be covert and inviting of corruption. This 302 report went on to say: "McDonald admitted that the Commission knew Resorts was dirty, controlled by organized crime figures, but gave them a license anyway." But what McDonald *actually* said on tape was quite different: "Where we would look for organized crime problems would be in the refuse, linens and stuff like that . . . we check out where the money comes from. We check out the people."

Then McDonald discusses a conversation he had had with a friend who had heard a radio talk show which discussed the Commission vote on Resorts: "What happened to the voting and the granting of the license and the guy on the other end of the phone says, 'yeah we knew they got that. Faked it. Passed and got their license. The commissioners were paid off.' And the news guy said, 'Really! Well how much did they get?' 'I don't know how much they got, but they're fixed for life.'" McDonald then says, "Geez, I wish to hell *I* was. This is a reaction . . . 90 percent of the [Resorts] case was innuendo and dealt with association out of the state, which we had to knock out before we could prove it. It was not there."

McDonald's denial of the radio talk show complaint of corruption in his Commission is clear ("Geez, I wish to hell I was"). His explanation about why Resorts got its license is equally emphatic: the Commission was unable to find proof of any wrongdoing. Exactly how the agent who wrote the 302 report managed to extrapolate from this conversation that McDonald "admitted" that he "knew Resorts was dirty, controlled by organized crime figures, but gave them a license anyway," is difficult to imagine.

The point of this contrast of perspectives is to point out the weakness in the government's predicate for pursuing McDonald further. Everything hinged on an admittedly corrupt, co-opted conspirator's accusation of McDonald's eagerness to be bribed. This occurred before the agent met McDonald. Now, in this first meeting, McDonald acts appropriately and with integrity. But, by this time, agent McCloud is possibly so contaminated by Errichetti's earlier report that he hears what McDonald said with a different construction than his words justify.

Good intelligence analysis at the FBI would have noted the difference between the reality of the actual conversation and the twisted 302 report. Good intelligence analysis frames multiple hypotheses and is not bound to a single theory of what is happening. It is not contaminated, particularly when the evidence is tape recorded, providing verifiable analysis. It would appear that the FBI determined to continue its investigation of McDonald solely on the basis of the agent's 302 report of the meeting of March 5 rather than on careful listening and analysis of the tape recording of actual event that the agent so inaccurately described.

On March 31, 1979, Errichetti pushed his plan to the next level. His old friend, McDonald, had been depressed about the recent death of his wife. Errichetti built on his friendship and McDonald's need for companionship to invite him to have dinner with him in New York. On the way, Errichetti mentions that he has to make a brief stop at an office on Veterans Memorial Highway in Holbrook. As he parks the car, Errichetti asks McDonald to come along with him. The visit will be brief and this way McDonald won't have to sit alone in the car. McDonald agrees to accompany Errichetti and they enter the office of agent McCloud, presumably the offices of Abdul Enterprises.

Unknown to either Errichetti or McDonald, of course, this meeting was being secretly video-tape recorded. Errichetti was right about one thing: the meeting was brief. It lasted only 16 minutes and 20 seconds. The audio and video quality of the recording were both exceptionally poor, making it difficult for the government to produce a transcript which recorded every word spoken. But enough was audible to get the gist of the sentences and to cause the FBI to believe that they had enough to indict McDonald.

A topic analysis of the conversation shows that there were 22 topics introduced. Three of these were introduced by McDonald. In one topic, McDonald asks McCloud if he lives locally, and also about the local airport and the industrial parks in the area. From what McDonald contributes to the conversation's topics, there is not the least indication of his intention to engage in anything corrupt. Errichetti controls the conversation, introducing 14 topics, and McCloud brings up five.

The video camera is crucial for the analysis of this conversation for it clearly shows the positioning of the three men. McDonald follows Errichetti into the room several steps behind him and walks over to the window and looks out while Errichetti and McCloud stand at McCloud's desk. There is the usual conversational small talk at the beginning about a speech on TV, about a *New York Times*'s article and about a visitor from Germany. At this point, McDonald begins looking at his appointment book and turns away from the two men, still at the window, as far away from the desk that he can get while still remaining in the same room. Errichetti then addresses McCloud specifically. At various points in the conversation McDonald is not visible at all, either hidden from the camera by the two men or, perhaps, outside. Noting his non-participation in the conversation, Errichetti then tells McCloud that McDonald was once the president of Esterbrook Pen Company. McDonald volunteers a few turns of talk about the history of that company, then introduces his topic about the local airport, then he turns toward the window once again.

Prior to the meeting, according to McCloud's FBI 302 report, Errichetti was to signal an exchange of briefcases with McCloud by saying "money for the future." This would trigger McCloud to put his own briefcase on the table, full of money, to be exchanged for Errichetti's empty one. As this was happening, McDonald's attention was outside the window. He introduces his third and last topic at this point, "Are you building industrial parks here?" McCloud says "huh?" for, clearly, McDonald was off topic. Errichetti had assured McCloud that McDonald was in on the transaction and an off-topic question like this was disarming to the agent. Sensing a problem, McCloud responds:

> *McCloud*:   Yeah. I hope that, Ken, I hope that there won't be any problem with out . . .

He never gets a chance to finish his sentence as Errichetti leaps in and says:

> *Errichetti*:   No, there's no problems.

Undaunted, McCloud tries to finish his sentence:

> *McCloud*:   . . . licensing or anything in, uh, in Atlantic City as a result of this.

Again, Errichetti answers:

> *Errichetti*:   Okie dokie. In regards to licensing, if I may just bring that point out . . . Just recently I talked to him on the phone, so there's no question about that. In regards to Guccione's thing, okay? . . . You're in first place.

During this exchange, McDonald's head is turned away from them. He is again examining his appointment book, facing the window. Errichetti then continues:

> *Errichetti*:   Now, that's the part, the part I told you about after I spoke to him (*gestures with his thumb over his shoulder toward McDonald*) in regards to that.

McDonald's head is still turned away from the conversation and he could not have seen Errichetti's gesture.

Noting this odd behavior on Errichetti's part, to gesture toward McDonald and to respond as though it were on McDonald's behalf, and also noting McDonald's absence of participation, McCloud then says:

> *McCloud*: Well, I'm sure that we're not going to have any problems after today as far as the T's are being crossed and the I's being dotted.
> *Errichetti*: No problems. The very simple part is the investigation of it ... Meaning that if you have a record in your past, anything that would prohibit you from your license. That's another story. Make sure your nominee's clean.

At this, Errichetti smiles and points to his briefcase and says, "That's what we discussed." Still not convinced, McCloud tries again.

> *McCloud*: As long as we have no problems at all with the licensing, as you say ... I have a pile of dirt unless I get that casino license. Because that's where the money is to be made and that's why we're all here today.

Meanwhile, the briefcases are exchanged and Errichetti offers a conversational pre-close (an indication that he is ready to leave):

> *Errichetti*: Jack, awful nice talking to you.

At this point begins 13 seconds of very confused and overlapped speech. Careful listening after dozens of replayings of the tape reveals the following transcript of those 13 seconds.

Errichetti	*McCloud*	*McDonald*
16:30 Jack, awful nice talking		
16:31 to you.	Okay Ken	
16:32		Jack
16:33	Okay.	
16:34		Good to see you and, uh,
	Thank you very	I'm sure
16:35	much Ken	

16:36		I'm sure we'll do alright, huh?	That if
	I don't		
16:37		Won't be any problems	
16:38	No problems		
			You're right
16:39			on the team,
16:40			You're doing
16:41		No problems	it the right
			way.
			I'm, I have
16:42			nothing to do
16:43			with that.

A great deal was made by the government of these 13 seconds. Note how the FBI's transcript of these 13 seconds was displayed:

Errichetti: Jack, awful nice talking to you.
McCloud: Okay ... Ken.
McDonald: Jack.
McCloud: Okay.
McDonald: Good to see you and, uh (*inaudible*)
McCloud: Thank you very much, Ken and I am sure that we'll do all right, huh? There won't be any problems.
McDonald: And I was thinking (*clears throat*) you're right on the team.
McCloud: No problems.
McDonald: You're doing it the right way. I have nothing to do with that.

The first thing that is apparent from the government transcript is that there is a disagreement about some of the words McDonald actually said. The government transcript does not allow for overlapped speech (people talking at the same time) and it reads like a play script, assuming that speakers take discrete and uninterrupted, full turns of talk. Life is seldom like this, however, since people talk over each other, interrupt and mumble. The advantage of the defense transcript, which I proposed, is that it is possible to see the continuous sentence that McDonald was uttering during the periods of McCloud's overlapping and interrupting.

The video tape also contributes greatly to our understanding of this conversation. It reveals McCloud's surprise that McDonald isolated himself from the most crucial parts of the conversation.

We see McCloud trying to draw McDonald back into it on several occasions, but to no avail. This crucial passage was the last of McCloud's efforts to get McDonald involved. The briefcases had been exchanged. McCloud's briefcase was, in fact, opened, revealing a great deal of currency. It is not possible to determine whether or not McDonald even saw the currency since he was facing the window, reading his appointment book and partially blocked by a camera angle that was apparently set up to view *three* men at McCloud's desk, not two.

The indictment of McDonald made much of the government transcript rendition of his alleged words: "And I was thinking you're right on the team." Unfortunately for the government's case, this is not what McDonald actually said. The words "And I was thinking" are nowhere to be found on the tape. The government missed Errichetti's "I don't" completely, which is odd since Errichetti's deep voice is very distinctive. The government also overlooked the social conventions of closing conversation. It is difficult to know exactly how much of the talk between Errichetti and McCloud that McDonald heard or attended to. But he did know that casino license was mentioned and he apparently heard Errichetti stress the need to keep it clean, using nobody with a record. McDonald also had to say something in response to McCloud's question, "I'm sure we'll do alright, huh?" Social convention requires an answer.

If one does not understand what is being talked about, one can use one or more of several available conversational strategies, such as:

1   Respond as though you really understood, even though you didn't.
2   Respond by saying that you do not understand.
3   Say something vague or general enough to satisfy the social requirement of response.

McDonald's response should be read continuously, from the start of his sentence, at 16:34, through the end of it, at 16:43, despite the interruptions and overlaps of both McCloud and Errichetti. What he says is:

1   Good to see you.
2   I'm sure that if you're on the right team (i.e. "if you put

together a group of umimpeachable persons") you're doing it
the right way.
3 I have nothing to do with it (i.e. "It's not my decision; it
depends on how you do it," or "I don't know what is going
on here but I want you to know that I am not part of it.")

At this point, Errichetti hands the briefcase full of money to his
chauffeur who had been waiting outside the office and McDonald
leaves for the car with the chauffeur. Errichetti says: "I'll be with
you in a minute, Ken ... I'll be right down." Then McCloud and
Errichetti continue their conversation alone.

Errichetti reports: "The money he knew, he's getting the money
right now. Joey's (*the chauffeur*) going to give him the money."
McCloud is not happy:

McCloud:	There's a hundred big ones in there ... What I need is the guarantee and that's exactly what I want and you got it and that's what I need.
Errichetti:	Forget the guarantees ... in fact, you and I got other agreements.
McCloud:	As long as anyone is happy, that's what.
Errichetti:	I'm happy and he's tickled to death ... we're in business.

The question in all of this, of course, is what, if anything,
McDonald agreed to. He was indicted for agreeing to accept a
bribe but, as indicated clearly above, he never did so. There is
considerable question, in fact, about whether a bribe was ever
offered. Clearly it was offered to Errichetti. Equally clearly,
Errichetti represents to agent McCloud that he personally had
made it clear to McDonald that he would get a bribe. But they
failed to get such agreement on tape. In fact, from the tape it is
obvious that McDonald did not know what was really going on.
The proof that McDonald *did* know what was going on would
be his receipt of the money. As it turns out, Errichetti had his
own scam in mind.

After the meeting, Weinberg and Errichetti met and split the
money between them, a fact which could have come out in trial
if the government agreed to permit Errichetti to testify. This was
unlikely, however, since Errichetti had been protected from having to testify in other cases where his words could have shown

the innocence of the accused, most notably Senator Harrison A. Williams.

There is, then, nothing in the government's tape-recorded evidence that could implicate McDonald in agreeing to accept a bribe. Indeed, a bribe was not offered. Briefcases were exchanged between Errichetti and McCloud, but McDonald was never informed about the meaning of that exchange and he was clearly not involved in it. The government's attempted case against him rested entirely on the word of Errichetti who, throughout the Abscam operation, had shown himself to be very, very guilty.

McDonald could not suffer the shame of being indicted for bribery when he had agreed to nothing more than to go to dinner with an old friend. His death soon followed, preventing the defense from presenting its case.

4

Agreeing

When a person asks us a question or makes a statement to us, we have a number of strategies available to us in our response. We can, for example, change the subject, disagree, agree, provide the necessary answer, or say nothing at all. To some, the notion of strategy implies a conscious, well-planned effort of some sort, like a move in a chess game or the sale of shares of stock. The fact that we do not think of conversational strategies, however, does not mean that they are non-existent. They may operate at such a rapid and seemingly intuitive level that we can scarcely believe that any conscious choice is being made.

To agree to do something, especially something very important, a speaker has a range of possible responses available. For example, consider the following range of answers to the question, "Would you like to purchase this car?"

1   Yes, indeed; I most certainly would.
2   Yes I would.
3   Yes.
4   I think so.
5   Uh-huh.
6   Uh.
7   (No response)
8   Huh-uh.
9   I don't think so.
10   No.
11   No I wouldn't.
12   No indeed; I most certainly wouldn't.

There are, of course, other possible responses to this question. The point here, however, is that our certainty about the intention of the person's responses is most clear at the polarities of this continuum. We are pretty certain about answers 1, 2, 11 and 12. Answers 1 and 2 contain multiple positives and answers 11 and 12 contain multiple negatives.

Answers 3 and 10 appear to be next most certain, containing, as they do, only a single positive and a single negative. Our certainty in these answers comes from the fact that the words used, *yes* and *no*, are what linguists call full forms. Full forms contrast with reduced forms of utterances which are thought to mean the same things. For example, consider the following ways of saying "yes":

1 Yes, indeed.
2 Yes.
3 Yep.
4 Yeah.
5 Uh-huh.

"Yes, indeed" is a double positive with a fully formed "yes." That is, the "yes" contains a consonant–vowel–consonant sequence that one-to-one reflects the letters used to spell the word in writing. The second answer, "yes," is not a multiple positive, but it is fully formed. The third response, "yep" is in one sense fully formed. That is, it contains a consonant–vowel–consonant sequence, but the last consonant is not a one-to-one correspondence with the fully formed, acceptably spelled "yes." The use of a "p" for the final "s" reduces the certainty of this response, adding a jauntiness in tone which calls in question the seriousness of the responder.

The fourth response, "yeah" is not fully formed. The final "s" of "yes" is deleted entirely, leaving only a consonant–vowel sequence. Finally, the last response, "uh-huh" is what is called a lax-token representation of "yes." The tenseness of the consonant–vowel sequence of the full form is relaxed (made lax) to a vowel–semi-vowel sequence of sounds.

The more certain and clear a speaker wants to be, the more that speaker answers in a way that is clear to number 1 on the yes continuum. These five "yes" responses are identified by their formal characteristics in table 4.1. With this breakdown, it should be clear that when we assess the agreement of one person to the question or statement of another person, we are most certain of

Table 4.1 Formal characteristics of five "yes" responses

	Multiple positive	Full form	Full but altered form	Reduced form	Lax form
Yes, indeed	X	X			
Yes		X			
Yep			X		
Yeah				X	
Uh-huh					X

their agreement when they use multiple positives and full forms than we are when they use altered forms and reduced forms. We can be very uncertain of that person's agreement when a lax form is used. In fact, we can be reasonably sure that an "uh-huh" response is not an agreement at all but, rather, a feedback response of the type discussed in chapter 1. That is, it does not mean "I agree." Instead, it can mean "I hear what you are saying;" "Keep talking;" or "I have not yet fallen asleep."

People get in trouble with the law when they agree to do illegal things. They may agree to purchase stolen property, agree to purchase drugs or agree to accept money for an act which they should not do. When the agreement is explicit and clear, there can be no question about the guilt of such people, but language is a very complicated coding system with many contingencies. It operates in a context and is subservient to the understandings of its users. In many law cases involving tape-recorded conversations as evidence, care must be taken to understand these contexts, to determine the most likely understandings of the speakers and, equally important, to comprehend the continuum of agreement markers noted above. Three case studies will represent the problems faced by the courts in trying to determine whether or not the target actually agreed to the illegal act for which he was charged.

Did John DeLorean agree to buy drugs?

Perhaps one of the most celebrated cases in recent years involved John Z. DeLorean, former vice-president of General Motors who resigned his post to build an automobile factory of his own in Northern Ireland. The British government agreed to finance the building of the factory as a way of providing employment in an area which was in a desperate economic condition. The factory was built and the first "DeLorean" cars were being produced by the factory when the initial funding ran out. DeLorean had been promised an additional 50 million dollars once the factory was built and effectively producing the cars. But the British government had changed and the then Prime Minister, Margaret Thatcher, was not inclined to honor any promises made by her more liberal predecessors. This left DeLorean in a difficult position. He tried desperately to obtain a loan of 50 million dollars to no avail and it was only a matter of time before he faced bankruptcy.

Meanwhile, the Drug Enforcement Agency (DEA) had been conducting an extensive and very expensive investigation of the entry of drugs illegally from South America into California. To this time, the major catch had been one James Hoffman, well-known swindler, con-man and convicted felon. Although the exact facts are not totally clear, somehow Hoffman suggested to the DEA agents that he knew John DeLorean personally and that he could "get" DeLorean for them. Under cross-examination by DeLorean's attorney, Howard Weitzman, the agent admitted this during the trial. The fact that Hoffman stretched the meaning of his "knowing DeLorean personally" is not surprising in light of Hoffman's history of perjury. In truth, Hoffman had once rented a house near DeLorean in San Diego for a very brief period, during which time Hoffman's son had been a playmate of DeLorean's son, Zachary.

Encouraged to make contact with DeLorean, Hoffman called him and suggested that he might be able to help DeLorean get a loan with a friend of his who was vice-president of the Eureka National Bank. This was good news to DeLorean and a two-month series of telephone calls ensued with a James Benedict, actually FBI agent Benedict Tisa, who posed as the bank's vice-president. During this series of telephone conversations, Benedict at first expressed strong interest in helping DeLorean obtain a loan. But after two months of delays, the agent finally told DeLorean that the bank could not provide such a loan, but that he and Hoffman had other resources and that they might personally finance the car company. Almost immediately, Hoffman met DeLorean in Washington, DC and, for the first time, explained that this personal financial resource came from a drug business that he had with banker Benedict. Hoffman offered that he and Benedict would either finance the loan to DeLorean from their drug business or else help to get other investors or loan sources for DeLorean's fast-sinking corporation.

One might be critical of DeLorean's actions once he learned about the origins of Hoffman's and Benedict's resources. Context is a crucial factor here, however, and it is always necessary for later listeners to the trial tapes to try to put themselves in DeLorean's shoes. His lifelong dream is 90 percent realized. One more small step will make it a reality. He sought legitimate funding elsewhere to no avail. Finally he gets word, out of the blue, from a former neighbor in San Diego, that the Eureka National Bank is interested. This is confirmed by the banker himself and DeLorean is beginning to see the light at the end of the tunnel. DeLorean has managed to delay the bankruptcy proceedings as long as possible. Unless he gets the money very quickly, however, he will be out of business. Now Hoffman drops this bomb on him. The loan money will be from a tainted source. DeLorean may have reasoned to himself: "I have two choices – bankruptcy or taking the loan from a tainted source. Does the fact that their money comes from drugs affect me? No, that's their problem, not mine. There is no other source of money available. Besides, Hoffman made two offers. One was to lend me the money from their drug business. The other was to help me find other investors. Therefore, it would be foolish of me to turn them off at this point. Why not find out more about these other investors? Then, if this doesn't work out, I can always let them lend me the money they make from their drug proceeds. I'm not involved in the drug deal; only as a borrower." Such reasoning is consistent with all of DeLorean's talk on the trial tapes.

One advantage that the FBI has over the people it tapes is that the silent, internal reasoning of the target is unknown. It can only be inferred from the target's own words and actions. Such inferences are hypotheses that can be tested against the evidence. The FBI's reasoning is much clearer, the FBI can have only one motive for taping in the first place: to capture illegality on tape. The FBI too has a hypothesis. First of all, the FBI agents hypothesize that

DeLorean is corrupt and that all they need to do is to capture evidence of this corruption on tape.

But where did the FBI get the idea that DeLorean was corrupt? What evidence is there in the taped conversations that would lead to such a hypothesis? In this case, none could be found. The FBI had only the word of James Hoffman, a convicted felon, an admitted perjurer, a notorious con-man. Hoffman told the FBI that in his earliest unrecorded conversations with DeLorean, he spoke of drug deals and that DeLorean expressed a willingness to be involved. But this is not on tape and there is no evidence that these conversations were even monitored by the government.

Whether or not the government was accurate in its hypothesis about DeLorean's culpability, the test of such a theory should be found in DeLorean's words and actions. If DeLorean was indeed corrupt, there should be evidence of corruption in what he says in the 64 taped conversations. What he says should be consistent with this hypothesis. By the same token, all of what DeLorean says on the tape should be consistent with the defense theory, if the jury is to believe DeLorean's hypothesis. Thus, the tape-recorded evidence in the DeLorean case became the testing ground of hypotheses or theories. The search became one of showing the consistency of his words with whichever theory one was trying to prove.

The actual trial of John DeLorean was judicial theater at its best. DeLorean's attorneys, Howard Weitzman and Donald Re, are justifiably given credit for one of the best defenses in the history of criminal law. They brought out inconsistencies in the procedures of the prosecution, forced an agent to admit that he had altered the date of some written evidence and generally called to question the ethics, if not the actual legality, of the government's procedures. These victories were major ones; ones which created such doubt in the minds of most jurors that even without testing the consistency of the tape-recorded evidence, DeLorean would be acquitted.

The point here, however, is that such a test shows clearly that the prosecution's position was without merit. Even more important, it is clear that the government intelligence analysis in this case was hopelessly flawed. One of the leading scholars in the field of police intelligence, Don R. Harris, in his book *Basic Elements of Intelligence* (The Law Enforcement Assistance Administration, 1976), observes that it is imperative that the analyst "formulate alternative hypotheses where there is limited information available."

This approach is most commonly used in the early collection of information (tape-recorded conversations, in this case) and it keeps the analyst from focusing on a single hypothesis, especially a hypothesis which may be in error. If the government agents had formulated more than one hypothesis, they might have learned that the test of consistency did not favor their "corruption" theory. Such a test would have shown that all of DeLorean's words and actions were consistent with the defense hypothesis previously shown (when we tried to put ourselves in DeLorean's shoes).

It would be impractical here to go through each of the 64 conversations to prove this point. Instead, let us take the videotaped conversation between Hoffman and DeLorean which took place on September 4, 1982. By the time the trial began, only four of the 64 tapes were considered crucial enough by the prosecution to be presented in support of their "corruption" theory. This tape was highest on their list.

Earlier we noted that topic analysis is one of the most important and revealing linguistic approaches to a conversation. Intelligence specialist Harris has observed that the role of summarizing intelligence information "reduces both the number of individual pieces of information available and the content of each ... to prevent the analyst from being swamped by data that are only marginally relevant." Topic analysis provides an outline or skeleton of an entire conversation which enables the listeners, whether the FBI intelligence analyst, the prosecutor, the defense attorney or the jury, to focus only on the topic introductions in a conversation, those things that were considered important by the person who introduced them. The topics a person introduces are a one-to-one reflection of that person's agenda and are a very strong clue to that person's intentions.

We noted earlier that most conversations contain portions of relatively unclear information. We also noted that in their efforts to capture corrupt language on tape, FBI agents or others wearing the microphone must be very careful not to be too blatantly illegal, else the target may be frightened away. On the other hand, even the FBI, in its guidelines to agents who are involved in covert operations, states that the nature of the illegality must be presented in a way that is clear and unambiguous. This tension between (a) being clear and unambiguous – and thus blatantly illegal – and (b) frightening the target off, with such blatant clarity, is a difficult one for all covert operations. If the FBI frightens off the target, the operation fails. If the agents are too ambiguous or unclear, the prosecution has a difficult time proving its case in court. The result is that the FBI regularly chooses to be vague and unclear, despite its own guidelines. In doing so, it relies on other factors to support its case. One of these, noted earlier, is the coloration of guilt: drugs are being discussed, foul language is being used, whether or not the target is present, criminal language and criminal acts are being employed, often by the agents themselves.

There is no excuse, however, for the intelligence analyst, the prosecutor or the jury to proceed with only a single hypothesis, one that supports only the "corruption" theory. They must also honestly and actively attempt to make the case of the defendant. This is important not only to be prepared to refute it, but also to determine whether or not the alternative hypothesis might better stand the test of consistency, especially when the evidence is not entirely clear. The first step toward hypothesis testing involves the tape-recorded words themselves. To determine clues to the intentions of the speakers and to avoid the "swamping" Harris describes, a topic analysis is called for.

Shortly before the meeting of September 4, 1982, Hoffman and Benedict had been trying to get DeLorean to scrape up some of the capital still available to invest in their drug business. As they put it, this would be an "act of good faith" on DeLorean's part. Again, putting oneself in DeLorean's shoes, one can see how DeLorean would want to avoid doing this if at all possible. After all, Hoffman and Benedict were still holding out the possibility of finding *other* people either to invest in DeLorean Motors or to provide him with a large loan. If DeLorean were to agree to their request and invest some of his dwindling capital in their drug operation, he would remove his last separation from their drug resources. It was bad enough to have to take a loan from a drug-based operation, but why would he need to do even this if another investor could be found? On the other hand, DeLorean could not merely thumb his nose at them and walk away. His last chance before bankruptcy resided in the hope of some unknown investor that they still held out to him.

The rules of the game were changing rapidly, however. First it was a legitimate loan from Eureka National Bank. Then it was a loan from Hoffman and Benedict's drug operation or their help in finding still another lender or investor. Now they changed even that. In order to get their drug operation loan, they ask DeLorean to put up some capital in good faith. "Better to avoid this at all costs," DeLorean reasons. "Better to defer them on this and hope for the outside lender or investor that they've been talking about."

Undaunted, Hoffman presses further for DeLorean's "good faith" investment in their drug operation. Finally, DeLorean tells them a lie. He explains that his remaining capital, some two million dollars, has been taken by the bankruptcy people in England, an untruth which is nothing more than a stall for time. Hoffman and Benedict counter this with a request for other evidence of DeLorean's good faith: stock in his ski equipment manufacturing company or titles to a few unsold DeLorean automobiles. DeLorean gives the appearance of consent to this plan since it will take several days to do the paperwork – another stall for time. Nothing is forthcoming from DeLorean, however, and finally, on September 4, 1982, Hoffman meets DeLorean to discuss the problem. The following are all the topics introduced in this conversation that the prosecution considered so crucial to his conviction.

DeLorean	*Hoffman*
1	greeting
2	lunch?
3	building
4	alternate Rockville
5	drink?
6	Thought we'd be together
7	Where do you stand with company?
8	delays
9 prior to interim financing?	
10	got group has ability – 30 million
11 They have an interest?	
12	Columbian folks
13	dope program
14	2nd level, 5 million

15		tell me how really pressured you are
16	It'll be dangerous	
17		800,000 investment returns 40 million
18		2 ways: (1) Interim financing, quicker,
19		or (2) or this, buy 100 kilos
20		300 investment, 14 million in 10 days
21		Biggest concern if you can't follow through
22		Absolute confirmation would be to invest it again
23		They want to make sure not to wind up short
24		JB handles money thru my boss – see him
25		He operates thru more than a bank also
26		He (JB) understands what's going on
27		He's not able to write bank guarantee
28	I'm getting money thru Irish group	
29	So its gotta be legitimate	
30		We don't want you not comfortable
31		You're not compelled
32		if you get money somewhere, else do it
33		either we go ahead or end
34	I'll get hold of them	
35	I want to do it, but they confirm it	
36	What should I do?	
37		Probably move in 2–3 days
38		I built other program in because within my control

39	first part of money has to be by Friday	
40		How long take to get confirmation of funds available?
41		I gotta go see wife, see Jim
42		My part equity, Vicenza next level
43		Your big deadline 28th or 29th?
44		Any way you can accelerate funding?
45	I'll hear from you Tues. or Wed.?	
46	I'd like to do this anyhow	
47		Not many people could pick up 30 mill in 3–4 days
48		Their rep. an American guy
49	Their interest as loan or equity investment?	
50	We'll be doing 400 mill by end of next year	
51		Their interest megamillion drug, coke
52		They have to move money every 90 days
53		So their interest is stock
54	We're accustomed to no disclosure requirement, off-shore trading Cos.	
55		desirable part facility to use
56		This a deal originally we weren't going to do
57	What's your opinion?	
58		Jim going over there, we'll sit here
59		Turn a few cars loose?
60		What are sales now?
61		Anybody with any interest is saying wait and see

62	media blitz
63	Jim hasn't been able to do anything
64	You got another place to go for credit now
65	We are ready to move
66	He has some other banking
67	people in Ireland know what's going on?
68	You ought to tell 'em it's craps game
69	nobody wants you not comfortable
70	From here on, dealings with Jim through Jim's boss and my boss
71	(*Telephone interruption JH on phone*)
72	You got anything Jim doesn't have?
73	Thatcher
74	We built plant in 2½ years
75	I think Sec. of State made deal . . . with that English to take it over
76	where will I get you?
77	close

The first thing to notice about this conversation is that DeLorean introduces only 18 (23 percent) of the 77 topics. (The words used to depict the topic initiations are the exact words used on the tape.) From this it is clear that the major agenda of this conversation is Hoffman's, yet DeLorean is accused of soliciting an interest in the drug business.

At issue in the September 4 conversation is whether DeLorean is agreeing to invest in the drug business, as a show of good faith, or whether he is still interested in a legitimate loan. The prosecution claimed that DeLorean was indicating an interest in investing in drugs. There is no question about the fact that Hoffman claims to be in the drug business (explicitly in topics 13, 19, 51 and indirectly elsewhere). DeLorean's only topic that even mentions drugs is his topic 16, in which he comments that "it" (the drug business) is dangerous.

The other critical topic is that of investment. That DeLorean believed Hoffman was referring to their interest in investing in DeLorean Motor Company (DMC) is clear in his topic 49. Hoffman's use of the terms *investment* and *financing*, however, are more ambiguously stated. What is missing is Hoffman's explicit words that *investment* means DeLorean's potential but currently stalled investment in their drug deal. Since DeLorean never promises this, he has no reason to believe that Hoffman's use of *investment* means DeLorean's investment in their drug deal.

Topic analysis is a very useful guide to the gist of the conversation. It points out the areas which require a more micro analysis, such as the reference to drugs and the references to investment in this example. Once the overall (macro) picture of the conversation is described by topic analysis, it is possible to focus on the crucial spots for a more detailed (micro) analysis of the responses made by DeLorean.

Obviously, speakers in a conversation not only introduce topics but also respond to the topics of other participants. Again, most people are unaware of the fact that they have strategies, consciously or unconsciously, of responding to the topics of others. There can be no question about the fact that DeLorean clearly understood that Hoffman was involved in the drug business. He had known this, in fact, for several weeks now. Of crucial concern, however, is the topic of "investment," especially as terms such as *investment* and *financing* are used in this conversation.

After the conventional small talk topics that are found at the beginning of most conversations, Hoffman asks DeLorean (topic 7) where he stands with the company. In topic 8, Hoffman points that there have been delays at his end. Since earlier conversation had been about a smaller investment in DeLorean Motors as an interim financing to be followed by a later, larger investment, DeLorean requests clarification about these delays. In topic 9 DeLorean asks if these delays will be prior to the interim financing. Hoffman then describes the financial resources of his group (topic 10). To this, DeLorean asks if this group has an interest in his company. At this point, Hoffman peppers the tape with drug references and DeLorean agrees that such a program is dangerous (topic 16). So far, so good for DeLorean.

Now Hoffman makes his big move (topics 17–27). He describes how the group operates and expresses strong concern (topics 21 and 22) that DeLorean "follow through" and "invest it again." There is not total explicitness in Hoffman's words, but there is enough to cause DeLorean to concoct a wild scenario about his also getting money through an Irish group (the IRA), a bunch of tough people who will worry, and possibly take drastic action, unless he is above board and legitimate in all his dealings (topics 28 and 29). This, of course, was pure falsehood but DeLorean's meaning came through clearly to Hoffman who offers to back off if DeLorean can get financed somewhere else (topics 30–33).

So far, then, we have Hoffman mentioning his drug business and how DeLorean should "follow through" and invest in it. But we also have DeLorean's clearest statement to date about how he is unwilling to invest. Instead of deferring and stalling, however, as he has until this conversation takes place, he now offers an explanation about why he cannot invest his money in their drug business: the IRA simply won't let him.

This invention also served another purpose, however: that of an implied threat. In a way, DeLorean was saying, "You mess with me and I might have to turn the IRA loose on you." At least one of these meanings came through to Hoffman, for he offers a choice: "Either we go ahead together, or end this all now." This too could be considered a threat by Hoffman to DeLorean, for "to end this all now" could be understood to mean that you can also give up any hope of our helping you get other investors or lenders. But, since this was left ambiguous, all we can really know is that head butted head. DeLorean, apparently bothered by the prospect of losing the last hope of a potential investor, turns to ambiguity himself in response to Hoffman's offer to end all this now. In topics 34 to 36, DeLorean offers to get hold of "them" (perhaps the IRA; perhaps Hoffman's people), says he wants to do "it" (either contact the IRA, go ahead with Hoffman's request to invest good faith money in their drug operation, or go ahead with Hoffman's earlier offer to find other investors or lenders). Equally ambiguously, DeLorean observes (topic 39) that he needs the first part (the interim investment by Hoffman's group?) by Friday.

Most conversations have their bizarre moments, when both
parties seem to be on different wavelengths for awhile. At this
point, this conversation enters such a zone of zaniness. Hoffman
seems to take DeLorean's preceding statement to mean that he is
willing to invest in their group (topics 40 and 44). But in topic
42, in between, Hoffman discusses his part of the equity, which
can only be understood to mean "portion of my group's investment in DeLorean Motors." This understanding is buttressed by
Hoffman's topic 43, which requests confirmation about DeLorean's
deadline for getting their investment in DeLorean Motors in order
to stave off the bankruptcy court.

DeLorean chooses to comprehend Hoffman's strange series of
topics as referring to Hoffman's investment in his company in
topic 45. But with equal zany ambiguity, DeLorean next says
"I'd like to do *this* anyhow." Once again, the vague "this" can refer
to a number of things, from checking with the IRA, to desiring
that Hoffman's group invest in his company, to desiring (but not
agreeing to) invest money in Hoffman's drug operation as an
expression of his good faith.

Hoffman then counters with another series of oddly disconnected
topics (topics 64 to 73), ending with a mention of Prime Minister
Margaret Thatcher, a topic about which DeLorean can never resist
comment. DeLorean spends two topics on his problems with the
British government, then asks where he can reach Hoffman and
the conversation closes.

The curious thing about Hoffman's last series of topics is his
domination and control, culminating with topic 70, in which
Hoffman presupposes DeLorean's agreement to put up good faith
money in their group and explains that from here on, DeLorean
will be dealing with higher ups in his group. In order to ensure
no contrary words from DeLorean, however, Hoffman brilliantly
brings up Thatcher, knowing full well (from all previous conversations with DeLorean) that this would be the topic, among all
others he had just introduced, that would capture DeLorean's
attention.

He was most certainly correct in this. It is a classic example of
the "bait and switch" tactic made famous by used car salesmen.
Hoffman knew full well that later listeners to this tape would
also assume that DeLorean's lack of disagreement to the other
topics would appear to be his acceptance of them. This "bait and

switch" technique, however, had already been used to good effect. The Eureka Bank loan was the first "bait." It was "switched" to a private loan from Benedict and Hoffman, along with the hope of getting other investors or lenders. This "bait" was then "switched" to an offer of investment in DeLorean Motors *if* DeLorean would also invest in their drug operation. These "baits" and "switches" are all thematic over the duration of the taping. More micro-level "bait and switches" are of topic shifts; there are many of these throughout the DeLorean case tapes.

Both DeLorean and Hoffman talk about "investments" and "financing" in this conversation but since Hoffman is not explicit about who is investing in what or who is financing what, DeLorean has to infer his intended meaning. Since Hoffman is wearing the microphone, he is, in a sense, making a documentary. On most occasions, it was entirely possible for Hoffman to be explicit when he was not. One can only wonder whether Hoffman, in his effort to produce a tape which would make DeLorean appear to agree to get financially involved in their drug operation, deliberately kept things as vague as possible. One classic way to do this is to refer to events, in noun form, without expressing the actions, or verbs, that require noun or pronoun explicitness. Thus, the following statement by Hoffman could be inferred in two ways:

> Either interim financing, which is still
> hopefully in place . . .

1 We will finance you on an interim basis, which is still in place.	2 You can finance us in our drug operation on an interim basis, which, we hope, is still possible for you.

Hoffman's careful selection of a nominal (noun) construction "interim financing" was totally naked of a main verb. Lacking a main verb, it also lacked the nouns or pronouns that main verbs require. This clever use of language enabled Hoffman to continue to walk the tight rope of ambiguity. In a sense, Hoffman had nothing to lose by being vague. If DeLorean made inference 1 and agreed, the prosecution could claim that he really was agreeing to inference 2. If, for some reason, DeLorean actually agreed to inference 2, the ball game was over for him.

This conversation contained many such ambiguous, noun-based statements made by Hoffman. The following are only illustrative. On August 31, Hoffman and DeLorean had the following conversation.

Hoffman: I think Jim should have some word today on that . . . interim thing. Things look pretty positive.
DeLorean: Then, uh, this interim thing, this is an individual or . . .?
Hoffman: No.
DeLorean: No?
Hoffman: No. This is . . . the group I told you about.
DeLorean: I see.
Hoffman: From down South.
DeLorean: Yeah 'cause we do need, uh, that's what we need right now . . . interim, the interim because time is of the essence.
Hoffman: We've got a time delay on my project. This thing would give, uh, provides some interim financing.

In this passage, Hoffman brings up the interim loan and DeLorean shows some confusion about it. He asks, in essence, "Will this interim loan be from one of the potential investors you've been talking about?" Hoffman says it will be from his drug operation group. DeLorean agrees that his company needs an interim loan. Hoffman's last utterance, however, is tantalizingly ambiguous. "This thing," to DeLorean, could only refer to the interim loan being proposed by the drug group to DeLorean Motors. Five days later, however, Hoffman twists the meaning of interim financing, as follows:

Hoffman: I ran into a few delays of my own and then in trying to put together this interim deal, that took longer than I figured and I've . . . got a couple of alternatives that I think are in place now.

Here Hoffman uses a phrase, which had one clear and specific meaning in the past conversations, to mean something different, to him at least, in this sentence. The phrase is *interim deal*. For one thing, Hoffman changes *financing* to *deal*, providing a more covert tone. Up to this point, this had meant only the first part of a two-part loan; an interim loan of a smaller amount which could keep the creditors away from DeLorean long enough for him to put together a larger loan. Such an arrangement was discussed with Jim Benedict of the Eureka Bank. DeLorean comes into this conversation with only this meaning in mind. The prosecution, on the other hand, claimed that Hoffman was referring only to drug deals here: an interim deal was a smaller transaction that DeLorean was asked to be involved in, and then there would be an even larger drug deal in which DeLorean would be asked to reinvest his "interim deal" earnings in the larger deal. The government had a serious problem with such an interpretation, however.

There was no previous reference to the prosecution's supposed meaning of the phrase. How then could DeLorean have comprehended Hoffman's meaning? In order for two people to understand the same thing, one of two things must happen. First, the words must be explicit and unambiguous. Secondly, if the words are not explicit, any inferred meaning must derive from what linguists called "shared world knowledge" or shared information. The simple diagram in chapter 1 (figure 1.2) can be applied here as figure 4.1.

Hoffman, being a clever con-man, carefully constructed his sentences so that he would get a favorable response from DeLorean. After all, Hoffman had promised to "get" DeLorean for the DEA. Up to this point, he didn't have much to give them. If he were to accomplish his promise, he would have to resort to cleverly constructed ambiguous sentences. The classic way to do this is to use terms which can be interpreted in different ways by the prosecution and the defense. Rather than to use explicit and unambiguous language, and rather than using language which derived from their shared knowledge of the world, Hoffman chose the deliberately vague approach.

Later in the same conversation, Hoffman uses this approach again:

Hoffman: There were two ways to do it. Either interim financing, which is still hopefully in place –
DeLorean: Yeah, that's the better way to do.
Hoffman: Or this.

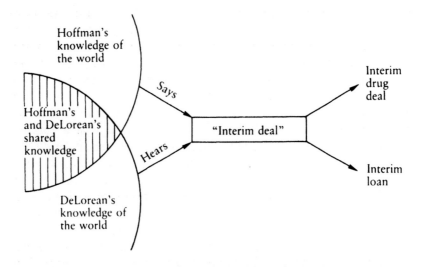

Figure 4.1 Differences in comprehension derived from separate
world knowledge in the DeLorean case.

Once again, "interim financing" to DeLorean can refer only to
his past efforts to get the first part of a two-loan sequence.
Hoffman even dangles a bit more this time as he contrasts interim financing with "this." Such a contrast can only mean that
"this" is the drug deal. DeLorean clearly votes for the interim
financing part of the contrast, as his words clearly indicate. But,
if the prosecution could make the case that Hoffman's earlier
"interim deal" really meant DeLorean's financial participation in
their first-level drug deal, and if the prosecution could convince
the jury that this is what DeLorean understood Hoffman to mean,
then the return to "interim financing" would also carry that
meaning.

What we have here is a clever effort by Hoffman to convert the
meaning of a harmless term, "interim financing," to an illegal
meaning, "interim deal." Once that meaning is understood, then
every mention of the original harmless term, "interim financing,"
would be contaminated and carry the illegal meaning with it.
This shift was accomplished in carefully plotted steps. For two
months, the term used was "interim loan," a loan that Eureka

Bank might make to DeLorean Motors. Clearly, there was nothing illegal about a loan and it would be ludicrous to try to claim that DeLorean might offer the drug group a loan. Hoffman's first step, then, was to substitute a vaguer term, *financing*. Financing, as a word, does not give any clues as to who is financing whom. Therefore, Hoffman reasoned, keep the concept *interim* and then slowly transition from *loan* to *financing*. Once that term was used, it would be ambiguous which way the financing goes. First ask DeLorean to invest in the drug business. Hoffman does so but does not achieve any commitment. Therefore, not being successful to this point, the good con-man tries his next trick: make it appear as though DeLorean did get a commitment. Get him to agree to *interim financing* without identifying explicitly who was investing in whom.

Hoffman did his best. He convinced the DEA and the FBI intelligence analysts that he had achieved what he promised. The grand jury was equally impressed and the case went to trial. It was only during the trial that Hoffman's linguistic skills came under careful scrutiny. Defense attorneys Weitzman and Re finally won their points and DeLorean was acquitted. The jury agreed and found DeLorean not guilty.

Did Hugo Forrester agree to purchase stolen property?

Jewelers are in a particularly vulnerable position by the nature of their trade. People often come into their shops to sell them gold and silver in the form of rings, bracelets, silverware and knick-knacks. Jewelers not only must accurately appraise the value and determine whether they can repair and resell for a profit, but they must also determine whether or not the property offered for purchase is stolen or legitimately owned by the customer. It is illegal, of course, to purchase stolen property.

Hugo Forrester was a California jeweler who had experienced legal problems in this area before and had been put on probation for a previous incident. In May of 1980, a man who had befriended Forrester in this incident showed up in his shop, claiming to have been in New York for awhile. This man, Davis Rubin, wore a recording device on several occasions and, as a result, several tapes were obtained by the local sheriff. At one point, Rubin introduced a sheriff's office employee, Alice Winston to Forrester as his girlfriend. She also wore a recording device in several visits to Forrester's shop. The tapes gathered by both Rubin and Winston provided the evidence used by the state to indict Forrester with agreeing to purchase stolen property. Forrester's attorney, Ephraim Margolin, then called me to assist him in the analysis of these tapes in the ensuing criminal case.

Since the taping was done during normal business hours, other customers came and went while Rubin's and Winston's recorders were running. Consequently, we have evidence of what goes on in an average day in a jeweler's shop. And since some of these other customers were also trying to sell Forrester jewelry, the tape provides interesting comparisons of Forrester's jewelry purchasing practice.

There were a number of questionable issues related to the tape recordings. At that time, the State of California did not have the subjective test of entrapment common in other states. This test essentially attempts to determine whether or not the individual charged with a crime was predisposed to commit it. In place of this subjective test, the State of California had an objective test that dealt simply with the nature of the government's endeavor. In particular, it asked whether or not an *average* law-abiding citizen, facing government inducement, would have been able to withstand such inducement. In short, if the government's agent pressures the suspect with overbearing conduct such as badgering, cajoling, importuning, or if the agent creates a motive through friendship or sympathy or offers exhorbitant consideration, or if the agent guarantees that the act is not illegal or that it will not be detected, the evidence is called to serious question. Under Californian law an expert can be brought in to explain what circumstances and factors might induce a normally law-abiding person to commit a crime.

Listening to the taped conversations, several linguistic issues were immediately clear, but the major question concerned Rubin's representation of the illegality of the transaction as clear and unambiguous. Contextual considerations were also critical. For one thing, some of the tapings were done in Forrester's small but busy shop. Customers come and go, the telephone rings, an assistant asks questions and Forrester must handle several things at once. It was also clear that Forrester made an inordinate number of requests to other speakers to repeat what they had just said, leading to the suspicion that he had a hearing problem. Attorney Margolin checked Forrester's hearing and verified these suspicions. These two contextual features alone were worth serious consideration, whether or not the entrapment test was applied. Did Forrester actually even *hear* the representations of illegality made by Rubin and Winston?

In their first meeting on May 19, for example, Rubin walks in, tells Forrester he's been living in Brooklyn and that he has some "stuff" to sell now and has a "bunch" more coming soon by UPS. Then, six minutes into the conversation, is the following:

Rubin: I bought a bunch of this stuff out East. It's stolen, you know, but I bought it back East and uh, I bought a lot of it. So instead of sending it to you by mail, I was worried that it would ever get here or anything. I bought this back myself and the rest is coming UPS this week and I'll have it here along with a lot of silver.

Forrester: UPS is not the greatest way to ship.

This passage was the cornerstone of the government's case and, on the surface, it might appear to be a strong one. Careful listening to the tape, however, revealed several important things. In his turn of talk, Rubin utters six propositions and Forrester responds to only one of the six, as follows:

Rubin	*Forrester*
1 I bought a bunch of this stuff East.	0
2 it's stolen	0
3 I bought it back East.	0
4 I bought a lot of it.	0
5 I brought it back myself.	0
6 The rest is coming UPS.	UPS is not the greatest way to ship.

If there had been a videotape of this conversation, we might be able to tell why Forrester does not respond to Rubin's damaging

assertion, "it's stolen." Perhaps he was occupied with something
else. Perhaps he was in another part of the shop. Perhaps he was
turned away from Rubin.

If we had only the transcript of these words, the case against
Forrester might seem even worse. But there was a tape to listen
to and this tape showed that Rubin's utterance of "it's stolen"
was embedded between three representations that he had *bought*
the stuff. This in itself does not deflect the fact that even though
he had bought it, the property was stolen by someone else. But
by embedding the fact that it was stolen in a more favorable and
seemingly legal context of his buying it, the listener who is not
ready to hear something shocking can easily overlook it. People
hear what they want to hear, as any communications scientist
will attest. They also infer from what they do hear a scenario of
logic which supports their initial understanding. Once listeners
start down a road of comprehension, they tend to assume that
the road leads where they think it leads.

But there is still more here. Rubin not only embedded these
words in the middle of more legal sounding words, as a kind of
camouflage, but he also distorted the pronunciation of "it's stolen"
in such a way that the camouflage was even more effective. He
did this in two ways. The normal stress pattern for such words
would show low pitch and stress on "it's" with high pitch and
stress on the first syllable of "stolen" with falling pitch and stress
on the second syllable, as follows:

$$\text{it's} \underbrace{\text{sto}}\text{len} \longrightarrow$$

Rubin did not say these words with normal pitch and stress.
Instead, he placed high pitch and stress on "it's" with low pitch
and stress on "stolen," as follows:

$$\overbrace{\text{it's}} \text{stolen} \longrightarrow$$

In addition to this reversed stress, Rubin reduced the pronunciation of the "l" in "stolen." When "l" is reduced, it is made less
like an "l" sound and more like a vowel, in particular, like an
"o" sound. Thus, "stolen" is made to sound like "stone."

A person with normal hearing, listening to this passage, might
not hear Rubin's words as "it's stolen" at all. In fact, it took

several careful listenings to make out what the government claimed was perfectly clear here.

Throughout this and other conversations in which Rubin spoke, there was no evidence of his having a speech pathology involving an "l" problem or a stress-pitch inconsistency. It was clear that he had manufactured it here as a way of preventing Forrester from understanding what he was saying but, at the same time, making a record on tape that could be used to convict him. We do not know where Forrester was in relation to Rubin's microphone when the utterance was made. But we do know that the shop was noisy and that Forrester had a hearing loss. More significantly, perhaps, we also know that Rubin's representation of illegality was camouflaged by propositional embedding, by reversed stress and pitch and by reduced "l" pronunciation. The government's "clear" evidence was not so clear after all.

Rubin returns to Forrester's shop two days later. After greeting Forrester, they are interrupted by another customer, and two telephone calls. When the customer departs, 15 minutes after Rubin arrived, Rubin again attempts to make a record of the illegality of his proposition while showing some rings to Forrester:

Forrester: Are they 14? Did you check?
Rubin: I did the acid to them. Check this out Hugo. I was curious about something. You know, this is what I don't, one thing that worries me, now this stuff is hot from back East or something, but how, there's no way in life that they can ever find out here, could they?
Forrester: No, but are you going to show where you get it?

Once again, things look bad for Forrester but the tape recording reveals some aspects that are not at all clear from the transcript. Rubin returns to his camouflaging strategy in his pronunciation of the key word, "hot." Normal, predictable English pitch and stress for this sentence is:

this stuff is ⌢hot ⌣from back ╱East ↘

That is, the words "hot" and "East" could be expected, in normal English speech, to be stressed and accompanied by a higher pitch than the rest of the sentence. In contrast, Rubin's spoken words display the following pitch and stress:

this stuff is hot from back East.

That is, stress and high pitch are on "this" and "East" with medium stress and pitch on "stuff" and "back" and low stress and pitch on "hot," the very word which makes the sentence crucial from the view of the prosecution. In other words, Rubin again camouflaged his intentions in such a way that it might not be noticed by a hearing impaired man in a busy, noisy shop. When stress and pitch are unpredictably lowered, the volume is also reduced. Although there is no good, non-technical way to describe this volume reduction, the following may at least illustrate it:

> *Expected, normal*: This stuff is HOT from BACK EAST.
> *Rubin's camouflage*: THIS stuff is hot from back EAST.

The effect of such a volume camouflage, of course, is to switch the stress from "hot" in favor of "this" and "East." By such a volume switch, Rubin diverts Forrester's attention from the crucial words to the less crucial ones.

But even Rubin's pronunciation of the key word "hot" is flawed. At this point in his sentence, he speeds up "hot from" and fails to articulate the "t" sound on "hot," yielding a highly speeded, low-volume utterance that is closer in audibility to "hafrom" than to "hot from," even when listened to over and over again.

Perhaps more damaging is Rubin's second effort to represent the illegality in this same conversation:

> *Rubin*:   . . . but I'm just wondering will they ever come in here, like will the police come in here, ask you –
> *Forrester*: From back East?
> *Rubin*:   Yeah, that's what I'm saying.
> *Forrester*: No.
> *Rubin*:   Oh, okay, good. If you [*inaudible*] stuff from three thousand miles away, you know, I'm, just sayin' I know it's stolen and I know this stuff was taken from a jewelry store or some shit.
> *Forrester*: Well, I don't want my girl to do anything with it.

In this utterance, Rubin is bolder. He pronounces the word "stolen" with normal intonation and with a fully produced "l" sound. The prosecution claimed that when Rubin said "I'm, just saying I know it's stolen and I know this stuff was taken from a jewelry store," their case was clear and the representation was unambiguous. But this is not as clear as it looks on the transcript. For one thing, Rubin pauses slightly after "I'm," as noted by the comma in the transcript. All normal conversations contain what linguists refer to as false starts. We all start a sentence, change our mind, stop in mid-utterance and go in a different direction. Couple this fact with Rubin's following word, "saying," and it is likely that some, if not most average listeners would think he had made a false start with his "I'm," then switched directions to a hypothetical. There are many ways to signal a hypothetical sentence. One is to say it performatively, such as "Hypothetically let's say x." Another way is to use conditional verbs such as "could" or "would," usually introduced with an "if" clause, such as, "*If* I know it's stolen" or "It *could* be stolen" or "What *if* it had been stolen?" Still another way to introduce a hypothetical is with the very word "say," as in "say it's stolen or something." When Rubin pauses after "I'm," as though in a false start, then follows with a clause beginning with "saying," Forrester is likely to have understood this as a hypothetical clause. This understanding is supported by Rubin's conclusion to his sentence, "or some shit." In the vernacular "or some shit" is roughly equivalent to "or something."

Often, in hypotheticals such as this, the hypothetical is introduced in the ways noted above and concluded with "or something," as in "What if it's stolen or something" or "say it's stolen or something." Forrester's responses, "Well I don't want my girl to do anything with it" is quite appropriate for such a hypothetical sentence. He does not want his assistant to deal with stolen property.

Forrester hears nothing from Rubin for over a month when, on June 25 Rubin returns to his shop with his presumed girlfriend Alice Winston, who is actually from the sheriff's office. Like the other earlier visits, this 14 minute conversation is frequently interrupted by other customers. It differs from the earlier tapes, however, in that Forrester's voice is frequently heard at some distance from the microphone and it is apparent from footsteps and other noises that he is often in distant parts of the shop.

The most crucial part of this conversation, from the prosecution's perspective is the following:

Rubin: We've got sterling silver and gold. There's, if she has
             I've been getting a lot of my gold and silver from her
             and I, you know, she, she's a maid, you know what I
             mean? So she, you know, one piece here, one piece
             there at a time out of somebody's house and, uh, she's
             got a badge (*laughs*).
Forrester: (*inaudible – at a distance*)
Rubin: Well what do you mean?
Forrester: (*inaudible – at a distance*)
Winston: (*inaudible*) that way they don't know (*inaudible*) think
             there may be, you know (*inaudible*) borrowed it ...
             just borrowed it.
Forrester: (*inaudible*)

There is no audible use of explicit words such as "stolen" or
"hot" in this passage. Instead, Rubin and Winston *imply* through
various words that the goods may be stolen. From Rubin's words:

• she's a maid
• one piece here, one piece there
• out of somebody's house

Forrester is to infer the connection and to understand that the
goods are stolen. When Winston says "borrowed it," the same
inference is to be made by the jeweler. These appear to be reasonable inferences that could indeed be made if Forrester had caught
Rubin's earlier garbled efforts at being explicit with his words.
There is every reason to believe, as noted earlier, that Forrester
did not catch this.

It also might be reasonable, even without Forrester's hearing
Rubin's "stolen" and "hot" in the earlier conversations, for
Forrester to infer something very gray about their activities if he
had, indeed, heard what they were saying here. The tape recording was of very poor quality in this conversation, as the many
inaudibles will attest. It is impossible to determine what Forrester
said since he was at such a distance from the microphone. The
fact that the telephone, other customers and other employees are
keeping Forrester very busy throughout the conversation, coupled with his hearing problem and distance from the microphone,
explains why his responses were inaudible. In fact, we do not
even know that he was responding to Rubin and Winston at all.
Anyone capable of camouflaging the illegality of his actions the

way Rubin had done earlier is also capable of simply making a record on tape here, one in which later listeners, a jury in particular, might overlook the fact that Forrester was not close enough to hear what they were saying on tape.

Another month passes before Forrester is contacted again, this time in a phone call from Alice Winston. Forrester does not recognize her name. She then identifies herself as Davis Rubin's friend. There is a long pause, then Alice repeats, "Dave." Forrester shows no sign of recognizing either Davis or Dave, so Alice goes on to explain:

> *Winston*: I have here uh two rings that I wanted you to look at and I just got 'em out of this guy's house, that I'm cleanin' . . . And uh I just kinda wanted to ask you if you could look at them for me.

Forrester agrees to look at them. Alice's observation that she got the rings out of this guy's house that she was cleaning would not be a red flag to Forrester unless he remembers who she is, that he has talked to her before, that he had heard what she and Rubin said a month earlier about her getting a piece at a time in her maid's work, and that he inferred correctly that "getting things out of houses" meant stealing. The likelihood of such a sequence is very low, in light of the tape recordings themselves.

Once again, almost another month goes by before Rubin calls Forrester and reports that he has a "couple pounds of really nice sterling silver . . . pots and stuff like that." Rubin says he can't bring it down himself but he'd like to send his friend, Mitch Johnson, down with it, but he'd like Forrester's check for it to be in his own (Rubin's) name. Then Rubin drops his bomb:

> *Rubin*: See, the thing is, with the stuff is that I, it was about two weeks old, it's hot, but it's about two weeks old, but I want the check in my name because that way I can guarantee that I'll get my money out of it. So if he comes down could you write it in my name?
>
> *Forrester*: Mmm. Yeah. I, I can, but I don't really like that uh whole background, you know.
>
> *Rubin*: Well it's, it's the stuff's nice and it's, there's, it's really nice. It's cooled off quite a consideration. It's there's no problem, you know, anything being, uh, you know, adverse with it or anything. It's good, you know.

Rubin then changes the subject back to writing the check in his name and the conversation ends.

Once again, the prosecution seemed to have the evidence it had been trying to get for three months. Rubin had said "it's hot" and "it's cooled down quite a bit." This time the terms of illegality were said on the telephone, not in a noisy shop where Forrester might not hear. Of these two representations of illegality, "it's hot" is considerably more devastating that "it's cooled down quite a bit," except for the fact that once again Rubin may have been trying to camouflage the word by embedding it in a series of five propositions and again, he reversed the stress and pitch of "it's hot," focusing on "it's" and barely uttering the word "hot." One of Rubin's most outstanding aspects of language style is his frequent use of false starts. The sentence in which "it's hot" occurs begins with six preceding false starts. Rubin cannot seem to get on track for what he is trying to say here. Visually, this sequence might be depicted as follows:

1 See
2   the thing is . . .
3   with the stuff is . . .
4   that I . . .
5   it was . . .
6   it's about two weeks old . . .
7   it's hot . . .
8   but it's about two weeks old . . .
9   but I want the check in my name –

With Rubin's reverse stress on "it's hot" and his embedding it in a sequence of false starts, the clarity of these words fades considerably. First of all, listeners tend to ignore or forget false starts since they do not contribute to the comprehension of speaker's words. They are, by definition, out of the listener's focus. Secondly, by reversing the intonation, the resulting sounds, if heard at all, sound more like the intonation of the utterance, "it's not," as in "It's not that I'm in a hurry."

Once again the government's evidence was faulty, largely because it was camouflaged beyond possible recognition of the target. It may have looked incriminating in the written representation of a transcript, but in tape cases, the transcript is not the evidence.

The tape is and the tape showed this evidence to have been faulty.

To this point then, every presumably inculpatory statement by Rubin and Winston and every alleged inculpatory response by Forrester was seriously and convincingly challenged. Each additional piece of the prosecution's evidence builds on the one preceding it, like a stack of building blocks. Take away the one below and the stack collapses. The prosecution was left with a single block, resting in the air and about to collapse along with the others, namely, Rubin's phrase, "it's cooled off quite a consideration." The first thing to notice is that Rubin, in typical fashion, embeds the phrase in a series of four propositions, as follows:

1 The stuff's nice
2 it's cooled off quite a consideration
3 There's no problem being adverse
4 it's good

Assuming that Forrester, unlike most people, is adept at processing several sequential propositions and responding to each of them, and assuming that Forrester, with his faulty hearing, actually heard all four propositions, the major clue to his comprehension and attention will be found in his response. He was being asked to purchase some goods and to write a check not to the person who will bring the goods in but to the person calling him on the telephone. Forrester has already indicated that he does not like to do this. For one thing, there is no way that he can tell whether the goods are as good as Rubin makes them out to be. This sort of thing simply can't be done over the telephone, sight unseen.

Forrester's focus in this conversation is on the potential problems he might have in paying Rubin's friend an amount which Rubin does not agree with. His response indicates this: "These kinds of conversations are not for a telephone . . . I'll do it but I, I don't want this to become a habit, okay?" The prosecution, of course, took this as evidence of Forrester's awareness of telephone interceptions, his desire to be covert and his understanding that the goods were stolen. Yet such an interpretation hinges on many things that are simply not grounded in the evidence, as noted earlier. The case was being prosecuted on camouflaged representations of illegality in a context in which it was not clear who was talking with whom or who was listening or even present, to a man whose hearing was deficient and who was surrounded by distractions of many types. He was then supposed to infer the covert intent of Rubin and Winston based on the few explicit references to "stolen" and "hot" that were themselves so camouflaged that even later listening to the tape required many listenings to reconstruct.

In the light of the California objective test of entrapment, it was maintained by the court that Forrester was not badgered, cajoled, importuned, offered exhorbitant considerations or guaranteed that the act was not illegal and the case went to trial. The issue then became one of fact, not of legal interpretation. At issue, quite simply, was whether or not Forrester ever agreed to purchase stolen property. The state's own tape-recorded evidence, as noted above, makes it clear that he did not so agree. In the end, the jury convicted on four counts and acquitted on two.

5

Threatening

Threatening is a speech act that differs from a promise in the following way. A promise is made by a speaker to do something for the hearer's benefit. A threat is quite the opposite: the speaker does something to the detriment of the listener. Furthermore, when one person threatens another person, he does not take the hearer's point of view, as with advice or warnings. Note the following contrasts for threatening, warning, advising and promising (table 5.1).

A promise, for example, commits the speaker to do something beneficial for the listener, as in "I promise to give you my inheritance." The perspective of the speaker is personal – what he or she will actually do. Advising, in contrast, has the listener's benefit in mind but is uttered from the listener's perspective, not the speaker's, as in "If I were you, I would change your will" or "You would be well advised to change your will." A warning shifts the perspective to the speaker, as in "I warn you that there will be serious consequences to you if you do not change your will." It is the speaker's knowledge that controls the warning, in contrast to advising, where the speaker's knowledge is present but the control is assigned to the listener. It is the listener's choice to do with as he or she wishes.

A threat, in contrast to the other speech acts noted, is generated from the speaker's perspective, is under the speaker's control and will lead to the listener's detriment. As such, threatening of life and other serious matters is considered a crime. Our society tolerates warnings, appreciates advice (doctors and lawyers are in the business of giving advice) and promises are acceptable as long as what is promised falls within the bounds of legality. Threats, however, are one of the most negatively received of all speech acts.

Table 5.1   Contrasts among threatening, warning, advising, and promising

	Threatening	Warning	Advising	Promising
To the speaker's benefit	X			
To the hearer's benefit		X	X	X
To the hearer's detriment	X			
From speaker's perspective	X	X		X
From hearer's perspective			X	
Speaker controls outcome	X			X
Hearer controls outcome		X	X	

Government agencies, such as the Social Security Administration, must walk a fine line in making sure that whatever advice or warnings they give to clients are not so strongly worded that they actually constitute a threat or are even perceived as being threatening. The public relations aspect of threatening is so strongly negative that it is not good practice for government agencies to do so, even if the results would prove beneficial to the client.

Threats become subject to legal dispute, however, when personal or physical harm is the logical outcome of the action. Law suits occur when one person uses language to threaten the well-being of another person. In the past, it has been difficult to prove that a threat was actually uttered. For one thing, the perception of a listener may be so skewed that a simple statement might be interpreted as a threat when one was not intended. If the case should come to court, the evidence is secondary, or reported evidence of what was said and, of course, subject to vigorous rebuttal or denial by the alleged offending party.

With the advent of surreptitious tape recording, however, actual words are preserved on tape for later analysis and they serve as evidence in the court, both for the prosecution and for the defense.

As we have seen with the speech acts of offering, accepting and agreeing, the actual event is made available and both sides must depend on it as the evidence. In this chapter, two cases involving the charge of threatening are discussed. In both cases, the prosecution was unable to support its claim and the defendants were acquitted.

Did Don Tyner threaten?

In September 1981, Don Tyner, an Oklahoma horse breeder, had three conversations that led to his arrest, indictment and trial for extorting two men, Vernon Hyde and Mike Blackburn. Both Hyde and Blackburn had been working for Tyner's organization and both were angry about shares in a horse which they believed that they had purchased but Tyner disagreed. Both had been telling other people that they were going to quit their jobs over it. Shortly before these conversations, they both quit.

In the morning of September 21, 1981, Hyde telephoned Tyner and the two got into a strong argument. Both complained about various injustices. This 30-minute telephone call produced 46 topics, categorized as follows:

Tyner's topics	*Hyde's topics*
Complaints about Hyde = 11	Expressions of fear = 8
Offers to settle dispute = 7	Disagrees to settle = 5
Company business = 6	The shares = 2
Small talk = 7	

From this simple distribution of topic areas we can get a profile of the agendas of the two men. Tyner is miffed about Hyde's resignation. He recognizes that their dispute exists and offers seven times to settle it. Hyde's largest topic area is to express his fear of Tyner and to turn down Tyner's offers to begin negotiations to settle their dispute. The three major areas of concern for this case are Tyner's complaints about Hyde, Tyner's offers to settle the dispute and Hyde's expressions of fear. It is instructive to recapitulate these three areas, along with the responses of the other party to each of these. Rather than to describe the details of the case further, I shall let the tape transcript speak for itself.

Tyner's complaint	*Hyde's response*
1 Mike filled my bookkeeper's head with lies.	0
2 I guess Lee's fixin' to quit. Ya'll have done a hell of a number on her.	0
3 Pruit told Lavonne that you told him you were leavin'.	I never said that.
4 Michael told us Saturday that you calculated your departure around getting your executed copies of the shares and making sure that your check had cleared the bank.	Well I don't think Michael said that.
5 You tellin' me you didn't calculate your departure around your check clearing?	What does it matter?
6 I'm gettin' more upset by the minute when I realize that you lied to me.	0
7 You deceived me. Why didn't you tell me you were gonna quit?	0
8 You're gettin' greedy.	Who is?
9 I cut somebody out of this syndicate to let you have two and you were deceiving me.	0
10 You ripped me off.	I didn't rip you off. I didn't take anything of yours and I didn't take everything of mine.
11 Did you work a full week? Did Mike? But no, ya'll got full pay checks.	

Huh? You didn't rip me off a bookkeeper?	I didn't take your bookkeeper.
12 Mike's a liar. He lied to Lee and he's lied to me. He's lied to you. He's lied to everybody.	
	I wonder what it was that convinced Mike to give away something worth 175 to 200 thousand dollars for nothin'.
13 Why do you have to be so greedy? Why did you have to calculate your exodus around gettin' your share?	
14 You only worked here a year. You're actin' like you've been here 20 years. Actin' like I owe you something.	0
	You don't owe me a thing and I don't owe you a thing.
15 You've stolen from me though.	No I haven't.
16 You've stolen from me.	No I haven't.
17 No. You've stolen from me. I call it thievery.	You know perfectly well I haven't. Us walkin' out there and deciding we don't want to work there anymore is not stealing.
18 I wouldn't tell me what to do if I were you. I told you what I'd do on that score.	You'd take it from me and give me nothing for it.

It is clear that Tyner is angry. Many of his complaints are simply not responded to by Hyde. Some are denied. To two of Tyner's complaints, Hyde responds with accusations (to number 12 and number 18). It is clear, however, that no threats are made by Tyner as he complains about Hyde and Blackburn.

In contrast to Tyner's complaints are his offers to get together
and negotiate a settlement of their dispute. These can be listed as
follows, again with Hyde's responses:

Tyner's offers to settle   *Hyde's responses*

1 All you gotta do is come
 in here today and we
 can ... get straightened
 out on everything and
 part peacefully.   How am I gonna part
              peacefully with this kind of a
              threat hanging over me?

2 I told you when I was at
 your house what I would
 do. And that's what I'll
 do. And you can come
 in today and we can get
 it done.   How do you expect me to
              walk into your office after that
              scene ya'll pulled with five guys
              out at Mike house?

3 I think the best thing
 you can do is settle this
 thing up, at my house or
 at the office, whenever
 you want to meet. And
 we'll go down the road
 peacefully.   You offered to steal one of my
              shares and let me keep one.

4 I told you how I'll settle. We could have it now, but not
              with you doin' what you're
              doin'.

5 Well then let's get it all
 resolved.   No. Let's call off these guys,
              these goons you got.

6 Let's get it resolved and
 we'll be, you know,
 taken care of.   And if I don't?

7 You see right now you
 can settle it peacefully
 and keep one share.   0

8	I will meet you by myself.	Yeah, I believe that.
9	Well you name the place, you can put it out 20 miles in the country.	I'm sure foolish enough to do that.
10	I'm trying to get you to sit down and talk and you won't do it.	I don't need the kind of talking that you gave Mike.
11	If you want to, fly out to Urschel's and meet out there and talk, we can do that too.	Well they can't stop me.
12	You know, there's a football field out at State U. We could meet there in the middle. You'd know I didn't have anybody with me. And we can sit down and talk about this.	I don't think I'd ever make it to the football field if I agreed to do that.
13	You want to meet out there at the football field, sit down and talk about this?	No.
14	I'll sell it for $100,000. I don't want the share myself.	Then why don't you offer for them to buy it from me.
15	I'm gonna sell the share for $100,000. And you can keep your share and when you get ready to sell it, I'll help you sell it.	I'll think about it.
16	We can settle this thing up and part peacefully and be no problems.	I'll talk to you Wednesday.

From the text it is clear that Hyde rejects most of Tyner's offers to get together and settle their dispute. He defers two of the offers, the last two, and responds to two others with accusations (numbers 3 and 5).

Hyde's major topic is to express his fear, largely through rather inexplicit complaints. These complaints are as follows, along with Tyner's responses.

Hyde' complaints	*Tyner's responses*
1 I feel left high and dry. I can't even go to my own house.	Well all you gotta do is come in here today and we can get it all straightened out and part peacefully.
2 How am I gonna part peacefully with this kind of threat hanging over me?	I don't know, Vernon. I've got to take care of business. You can come in today and get it done . . . get it straightened out.
3 You offered to steal one of my shares and let me keep one.	I didn't offer to steal it. It's not your share.
4 We could have it now, but not with what you're doin' . . . This threatening stuff.	Then let's get it all resolved.
5 Let's call off these goons you've got.	Let's get it resolved.
6 I don't think I'd ever make it to the football field.	Well I don't know. But you know, by the way, have you talked to Hudibey about that deal?
7 Don't send your gorillas over to my house.	I don't have any gorillas.

8 You'd take it from me
   and give me nothin' for it.   I'll sell it for $100,000.

By now it should be clear that Hyde's major goal in this conversation is to imply that Tyner had the ability to set his "goons"
on him. This appears to be part of what the threat indictment is
all about but, as yet, there is only inferential evidence, and that
is from Hyde's words, not Tyner's. Tyner denies having gorillas
and he denies stealing anything of Hyde's (numbers 3, 7, and 8).
Tyner responds to four of Hyde's fear-filled complaints by offering
to settle their dispute (numbers 1, 2, 4, and 5). To the one other
complaint, Tyner discusses company business (number 6).

Later the same day, Mike Blackburn wears a microphone as he
visits Tyner in Tyner's office. This nine-minute conversation is, at
best, a vivid argument, but not a rational one. A reasoned argument is one in which the participants hold different positions
or understandings and try to convince each other of the correctness of their own positions. To do so, they offer new information, clarify and present evidence to support their views. Simply
rejecting the other person's position is not good argumentation.
An ineffective presentation is one in which the participants simply
utter their own propositions without evidence and then repeat
their own propositions over and over. Such an approach tends
to sound more like a playground argument than one that might
be expected between mature adults. This conversation cannot be
described as an adult argument. It's structure is irrational and
non-substantive and looks like this:

Assertion by first person	Intensified assertion by second person
More intensified assertion by first person	Even more intensified assertion by second person

Such a structure replaces logical or factual argumentation with
emotional, personalized (*ad hominem*) issues and shouting. The
best insulter may be thought to be the winner.

The conversation contains 31 topics; 22 by Blackburn and nine by Tyner. Tyner's topics are to remind Blackburn that the deal had been made, to accuse Blackburn of lying and to ask Blackburn to leave (three times). Blackburn's topics center around accusing Tyner of "setting him up," "pulling games," and expressing his fear of being harmed by Tyner (seven topics). Blackburn's alarm for his life is expressed to Tyner 17 times altogether. Tyner responds by denying that there is any reason to be alarmed (seven times), by telling Blackburn to leave (four times) and by giving no response at all.

Blackburn's complaints take the form of accusations. The reason people accuse are to elicit confirmation or denial or to arouse a strong emotional response such as anger or fear to the extent that the accused person might lose control. These complaints, along with Tyner's responses, are as follows:

Blackburn's complaints	*Tyner's responses*
1 I was under duress.	I don't care what Vernon told you.
2 I don't appreciate you settin' me up like that.	0
3 I don't know why ya'll trying to pull these games.	It ain't games.
4 You'd have one hurt over just one little ol' share.	I wouldn't have you hurt, Michael.
5 You were gonna have me killed over one share.	Why don't you just leave?
6 I signed under duress.	No, I don't think there was any duress.
7 You just want to fuck me out of this money don't you.	Nope.
8 If I have to hire me a body guard to take care of me, I'll do it.	You can't hire enough body guards to take care of you Blackburn.

9 Well you were gonna sell it under the table.	No, no, no, no, no.
10 I've seen too many of 'em done that way.	You haven't seen shit, man.
11 Don't send David over to set me up.	Just leave.
12 You accosted me in my own home.	No I didn't accost you.
13 You made it appear that you would if I didn't do what you told me to do.	No.
14 If you'd treat people the way they ought to be treated.	Oh, have I mistreated you, poor little baby.
15 Well I can hide where he can't find me.	You can't hide forever.
16 You don't scare me Don Tyner.	Well then just leave, baby.

Blackburn's complaints are about being cheated, signing something under duress, about past threatening acts against him and about potential future threatening acts. Tyner responds by denying Blackburn's propositions (ten times) and by telling Blackburn to get out of his office (five times).

If the government were to try to make a case for threatening in this conversation, such a case would have to be based on two sentences spoken by Blackburn:

- I'll have to hire me a body guard.
- I can hide where he can't find me.

Note that Tyner denies all accusations of threatening in the past. Now Blackburn points to future possible threats. The one-upping argument style characterizes this conversation and Tyner's responses to these two potential future threats is to one-up Blackburn's assertion with his own stronger response, as follows:

- You can't hire enough body guards to take care of you, Blackburn.
- You can't hide forever.

During the trial itself, the prosecution attempted to make much of these Blackburn–Tyner exchanges, as serious threats on the life of Blackburn. Contextually, such a position made little sense in that Tyner had a legitimate complaint against Blackburn's past activities, but he emphatically denies ever having threatened Blackburn in the past. The best that the prosecution could come up with was these implied fears of some future danger uttered by Blackburn along with Tyner's one-upmanship style of response. Note, however, that Tyner does not explicitly promise any future action. He says "You can't hire enough body guards" and "You can't hide forever." No statement of agent is made, such as "*I* will get you" or "You can't hide from *me*." All is vague and structurally appropriate to an angry argument between two people who have chosen not to argue by fact or logic. It is, indeed, little more than a shouting match.

On the next day, September 22, 1981, Tyner has a six-minute meeting with Hyde. Hyde requested the meeting and Tyner's first utterance is "What do you wanna talk about?" Hyde responds with the ostensible reason ("I wanted to give you your keys and power of attorney"), but leaps right into the familiar accusatory complaints. Tyner ignores these and brings up a couple of company business items that were unresolved and then says "I still can't figure out why you left bitter." Hyde then makes four consecutive accusations:

1 Because you showed up at my house and threatened me and Mike.
2 Are you still gonna try to take these shares away from me?
3 Nothin' made me any sicker than this threatening stuff.
4 I told Dan that you had threatened me and Mike.

Tyner denies the first accusation, then asks Hyde "What do you want to do on those shares?" When Hyde responds with more accusations of past threats, Tyner first denies this then tells Hyde, "Okay, you done fucked up, baby," signalling that he is finished discussing this matter. Then there is a pause, and Tyner asks:

Tyner: How's David?
Hyde: Do what?
Tyner: How's David?

Hyde: You mean my son?
Tyner: Yep.
Hyde: Don, don't threaten my son. Do a lot of things but don't
          ever threaten my son.
Tyner: I didn't threaten anybody. I just said, "How's David?"

At this point, the conversation ends and they part company.

The tape-recorded evidence produced by the government in its case against Don Tyner, then consisted of several reports of past threats by Tyner to Blackburn and Hyde but denied by Tyner; several potential threats feared by the two men; and one alleged current threat noted immediately above. Thus, there were three kinds of threats: past, future and current. To the accusations of past threats, Tyner denies vehemently. To the possibility of future threat events, Tyner either denies or ignores them as irrelevant and silly.

There was not a great deal that the prosecution could do with these past and future threat allegations since they were not tape recorded or apparently even witnessed. Instead, the government chose to use these past and future threat allegations as the basis for Hyde's inference that when Tyner asked about Hyde's son, David, what he was actually doing was implying a threat.

In an effort to bolster their case against Tyner, the prosecution called on Dr Murray Miron of the Psycholinguistics Center in Syracuse, New York. Dr Miron serves as a consultant to the FBI on matters relating to threats. His work typically involves evaluating the seriousness of thousands of anonymous telephone calls about bomb threats or written notes along the same lines. It seems that Miron's assessment of these messages enables the FBI to decide which messages to follow up on and which to ignore. Dr Miron's opinion was that Tyner's "How's David?" question was a serious and real threat on David's life.

Meanwhile, the attorney for Tyner, D. C. Thomas of Oklahoma City, called on me to analyze all three conversations, using speech act and discourse analytical routines. As usual, the context of the conversations gives many clues to their meaning which the words alone may not make clear to later listeners, such as juries. It was the case, for example, that Tyner knew Hyde's son David and had, in fact, taken David to horse races and other events.

It is also the case that the structure of conversation gives clues to the contextual meaning. By the time Hyde produced his fourth accusation, Tyner had had enough. He had denied the other accusations but by now he was tired of doing so and he terminates the topic, and the conversation, with his words, "Okay, you done fucked up baby." After a pause, Tyner then begins his conversational pre-close, changing Hyde's topic completely and asking about David. Had Hyde taken this as a real request about David, he might have responded "Fine, thanks" and they would have closed the conversation off with their goodbyes. When Tyner hears that Hyde took this as a threat, he denies it and apparently leaves. His voice fades, indicating that he was moving away from the microphone worn by Hyde and no goodbyes can be heard.

Genuine and explicit threats can be uttered in several ways. They can be said performatively, including specific reference to their threatening nature, as in "I threaten you with death." Or they can be explicitly threatening without the performative verb (a verb which defines the speech act), as in, "I'm gonna kill you if you don't do this." There can be no question about the threatening nature of either of these examples.

When threats are uttered indirectly, however, considerable ambiguity may result. For example, a person might say nothing more than "I don't like what you're doing," and listeners may infer that this is a threat on their life. Such an inference may or may not be true. The words themselves do not make this clear.

When this happens, linguists look to the immediate context for further clues. If the same speaker has just said "Someday you're going to find yourself in the hospital," then there might be some basis for thinking that "I don't like what you're doing" can be construed as a threat. This is the case because the latter sentence adds the agent, the speaker in this case, as the purveyor of the mayhem.

With this in mind, let us return to the "How's David" utterance made by Tyner. As noted earlier, Tyner had just refused to deny Hyde's accusations any longer. This was followed by a pause in the conversation. Then Tyner asks the question. There is nothing in the immediate context of this conversation to suggest that "How's David" is connected with Tyner's words, even inferentially. The difference in perception of these words may be shown in figure 5.1.

It is not uncommon for such misunderstandings to occur in

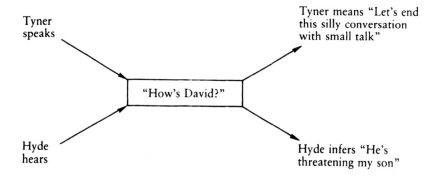

Figure 5.1   Differences in perception of Tyner's words
"How's David?"

everyday conversation. It happens to everyone. They usually grow out of different schemas, or frames of mind of the two participants. Examining Tyner's topics throughout the three conversations we find his major, recycled topic to be "Let's get together and resolve this disagreement." Hyde's and Blackburn's major, recycled topics are their fear and accusations. From these recycled topics, we can understand the agendas, schemas, or frames of mind of the parties. Tyner produces no threats in any of the conversations to this point and he consistently denies that he has made any threats before these conversations or that he will make any threats in the future. There is, therefore, no immediate or longer-term evidence that the meaning of "How's David?" can be anything other than what it says, a request about the well-being of Hyde's son.

Did Tyner threaten and thereby extort Hyde and Blackburn? The linguistic analysis of these tapes does not reveal any such threats. The jury agreed and acquitted Tyner of all charges.

Did Al Wash and George Malina threaten
Gary Barnhart?

A somewhat different type of threat event was alleged to have taken place in Dallas in the spring of 1984. Gary Barnhart owed

$20,000 to various people and one day he met three men in a restaurant. The meeting was not tape recorded but Barnhart claimed that out of the three, a large black man showed him his gun and put pressure on him to pay up.

Barnhart left the restaurant and went straight to his attorney who advised him to telephone one of the three men, Tony Natile, and to recapitulate the restaurant meeting on tape. On March 31, 1984, Barnhart made the call to Natile and expressed his fear: "The other day at lunch, I couldn't eat all day ... I was scared shitless." Natile, who also owed a great deal of money, responded by saying that he had problems sleeping and was also worried.

They both had reason to be scared since they were in debt and about to be foreclosed, but to this point, in the conversation, it is not clear that Barnhart is referring to any fear of guns or personal harm. So Barnhart clarifies: "I mean, I'm just sort of upset that they had to come in with guns in front of your kids and take you out of your house."

Natile:	Just one.
Barnhart:	Just one gun?
Natile:	Hell no. *(laughs)*
Barnhart:	Which one? The big black guy?
Natile:	That's right. *(laughs)*
Barnhart:	He's scary.
Natile:	You don't have to tell me. *(laughs)*
Barnhart:	I mean I would think they would trust you enough to where you could drive over there on your own without him using a damn gun on you.
Natile:	To the point of you know, after all of this time where he says, "No more."

Several things are odd about this exchange. Why is Natile laughing during his turns of talk? Is he not taking Barnhart's fear seriously? And why does Natile deny that in an earlier incident, they pulled a gun on him then seem to go along with Barnhart's "without him using a damn gun on you." Careful listening to this tape reveals that while Barnhart was saying the words, "using a damn gun on you," Natile has already started his own utterance: "To the point of, you know." They are talking at the same time and it is unlikely that either speaker actually ever heard what the other was saying. Then Barnhart comes back to the topic once again:

Barnhart: Did you see how scared I was? I was shaking my ass off.
Natile: I know, I know. *(laughs)*
Barnhart: I about had a heart attack.
Natile: I know. *(laughs)*
Barnhart: I downed the rest of my wine quick.
Natile: See, I had already been through that part. *(laughs)*
Barnhart: Gah! I mean, did your son not scream and run when they pulled the gun on you?
Natile: No, no, no.

Again, Natile seems to think this all rather humorous. When he says, "I had already been through that part," he was referring to an earlier confrontation in which he was told that he had to pay up the money he owed, not to the incident at the restaurant where the brunt of the confrontation was on Barnhart. To Barnhart's reference to a gun being pulled on Natile, Natile says only "No, no, no." This vague response leaves open the possibility that Natile was referring either to the fact that his son did *not* scream and run or to the fact that no gun was pulled. The latter meaning is consistent with Natile's earlier response of "Hell no" to Barnhart's question, "Just one gun?"

At issue here is whether or not anyone had ever pulled a gun on Natile and, for that matter, whether or not anyone had ever shown Barnhart a gun in the restaurant meeting that was not taped. Certainly Natile does not confirm this, although he *does* confirm the fact that Barnhart appeared to be scared.

The government's case seems to get more serious later in this telephone call when Barnhart continues:

Barnhart: Well, hopefully these guys won't kill me on Tuesday. How many hours do I have to live after Tuesday?
Natile: I don't think many.
Barnhart: Really?
Natile: I don't. I mean that I got the same problem.
Barnhart: I mean after they kill me, they're gonna kill you.
Natile: I don't know what they're gonna do. Do you think you're gonna have trouble getting that money?

On the surface it appears that both Barnhart and Natile believe that someone is going to kill them because they "have the same problem" (i.e. they owe money). It is clear that Barnhart believes that "kill" means to make dead. But does Natile mean the same thing? His laughter throughout the first part of this conversation would not indicate such a fear. Nor does the following exchange:

Barnhart: Okay. Shit. I'm just afraid I'll turn around and they're gonna put a bullet in my back.
Natile: No, no.
Barnhart: Do you want to go in there with me?
Natile: Yeah.
Barnhart: Okay.
Natile: That's even better.
Barnhart: You make me feel better already.
Natile: Yeah. I'll do that. No, what the hell.
Barnhart: Okay.
Natile: Alright, let's do that. Listen, I got to take this other call.

Again, Natile's responses to Barnhart's fear of being killed may seem inconsistent. Natile seems to be saying that he doesn't think Barnhart has many hours to live after Tuesday, the day the money is due. In contrast, Natile denies that "they" are going to shoot Barnhart and agrees to go with Barnhart to the meeting with the person to whom they owe the money.

If Natile feared for his own life or if he feared that a murder might take place, it is thoroughly inconsistent that he would agree to go with Barnhart to his day of reckoning. It is further inconsistent that he would shrug it off with "No, what the hell." And if Natile were really thinking about life and death issues, it is strangely inconsistent that he would then suddenly change the subject to another telephone call he had coming in. The question, then, is what did Natile mean when he told Barnhart that he didn't think Barnhart had many hours to live after Tuesday? Did he believe that Barnhart intended "kill" to mean "to make dead?" Or did Natile understand Barnhart's "kill" to be a metaphorical representation of the amount of extension time Barnhart might be able to get on repaying the money he owed?

This is a classic instance of where *contextual* meaning has more power and relevance than individual word meaning. It is common in English to utter sentences like: "I'm going to get killed on my History test" or "The Orioles are going to kill the Yankees tomorrow." When a loan is called in and the person owing the money wants a time extension to pay it back, the lender may also "kill" the borrower if he is not able to repay it on time. This does not mean to "make him dead" physically or explicitly. Instead, it refers to some adverse conditions such as increased penalty payments or interest rates, prohibition from future loans or business transactions or other possible outcomes. The metaphorical use of "kill" is widespread and common.

Contextual evidence that Natile took Barnhart's "kill" as metaphor can be found in Natile's responses themselves, as follows:

Barnhart: I mean after they kill me, they're gonna kill you?
Natile: I don't know what they are going to do. Do you think you are going to have trouble getting the money?
Barnhart: I'm doing everything I can.
Natile: But you're not getting it?
Barnhart: No, I am generating some. I'm not gonna tell you that I am generating it all, 'cause then I might not.
Natile: That's right. *(laughs)*

Natile's topic and focus is clearly the money that Barnhart owes and whether or not he has the ability to pay it back to the person to whom he owes it. Natile does not much like Barnhart and he laughs often at Barnhart's predicament, particularly at how ludicrous Barnhart looked when he was scared in the restaurant meeting. All evidence points to Natile's perceiving "kill" to be a metaphor, a way of Barnhart expressing how angry the man would be when he showed up without the money to repay him.

But, later, when Barnhart makes his use of "kill" so explicit that it could not be misunderstood as a metaphor and clearly meant to shoot dead ("put a bullet in my back"), Natile quickly and clearly denies that any such thing could happen. He says "no, no" and volunteers to go with Barnhart to the meeting with the man he owes the money.

Three days later, on April 3, 1984, Barnhart tape recorded a meeting with Al Wash ("the big black guy" mentioned in the earlier telephone conversation) and George Malina. These two men were alleged to be the ones who were extorting and threatening Barnhart in the earlier, untaped meeting.

This tape recording was of extremely poor quality. No transcript was offered by the prosecution but it was claimed, by Barnhart, that it contained numerous threats and was full of angry conversation. Attorney Steve Sumner, who represented Al Wash, a former Houston Oiler professional football player who had been a sheriff's deputy for six years and was now a private investigator, called me to analyze these conversations. The first step was to have the tape enhanced, a technical procedure by which certain sound frequencies are adjusted so that the speech is more audible. Small improvements in audibility can be achieved with such a procedure, providing that the external noise, such as the clatter of dishes in a restaurant or background music, does not operate at the same sound frequencies as the voices on the tape. Since the technical quality of this particular tape was so poor, the acoustics engineer, Frank M. McDermott, requested permission to take his own copying equipment to the FBI office and make a fresh copy of the original tape. He did so and the result was astounding. From the enhanced copy of the tape of this meeting, we were able to produce a transcript which contained enough of all sentences uttered to get the gist of the conversation.

The first notable conclusion that this permitted was that there was no argumentative talk in this tape and that there were no indications of threatening or extortion. The second conclusion was that the tape copy originally given to the defense by the FBI stopped part way through the conversation. McDermott's enhanced copy, the one he obtained by going to the FBI office and making his own copy, contained a great deal more conversation that took place after the first copy had been cut off.

The third notable conclusion was that at the end of the McDermott copy, there was another two minutes of very clear and audible conversation between Barnhart and two unidentified males who were later determined to be the FBI agents in charge of the case. Among other things, the agents told Barnhart:

• You talk too much, man. We want *him* to talk.
• We're not going to bust them now.

To this, Barnhart objects strongly, "Then they're gonna know I did it." To this, the agent says, "Yeah, we're gonna get those fuckers."

The significance of this clear passage at the end of the tape cannot be underestimated. When the enhanced tape was played for the jury and they were able to follow along with the transcript

I prepared from the enhanced, and now complete, tape, they could see that there were no threats, no arguments, and no extortion. Even more significant, they could hear the complaint of the agent at the end that Barnhart had done a poor job by talking too much himself.

It was also clear that the agent felt that this conversation had not done the intended job of capturing illegal words on tape. The effect on the jury of hearing the agent say, "We're gonna get those fuckers" was considerable. The government's case quickly crumbled from its own evidence. The accusation of threatening could be supported neither by the actual words of Malina and Wash nor by the retelling efforts of Natile in the telephone conversation. Wash and Malina, were acquitted while Natile was found guilty on a minor charge.

6

Admitting

When people admit something, they report things that they have been involved with – things that they have done, where they have been, who they have talked with, how they have done things. In this regard, admissions sound a lot like reporting personal facts. But admissions are also more than this: people report the facts about things that they really should *not* have done. An admission differs from a simple report of fact in the wrongful, bad, erroneous or illegal nature of the event being reported. If a person were to say "I got up at 7am today," it could not be considered an "admission" unless there was some reason why it would cast aspersions on the speaker to report this. Perhaps the person had said earlier that he had got up at 5am. Now, after his boss questions him about why he was late for a job that began at 6am, he says, "I got up at 7am." What at first seems like a simple report of a rather dull fact now becomes an *admission* of why he was late. The context determines whether a statement is an admission or not.

Like many other speech acts, admissions may be accomplished in many ways. A speaker can use the word *admit* in the admission, as in "I admit that I got up at 7am." Linguists call such an expression a "performative verb" because the word *admit* performs the act that the sentence expresses. More often, however, people admit more indirectly, largely because admitting something is not an easy thing to do. Notice the following ways that an admission can occur following the boss's questioning, "Why were you late for work today?"

1   "I admit that I overslept" (performative).
2   "I slept till 7am" (indirect).

3 "I missed my bus" (indirect).
4 "I was here as soon as anyone else" (offers an excuse, but still contains an indirect admission).
5 "My alarm clock didn't go off" (offers an excuse, but still admits).
6 "There's no excuse for it" (offers no excuse but still admits).
7 "I wasn't late today, but I left early" (does not admit guilt charged but does admit something else).

Did Larry Gentry admit to foreknowledge of a murder?

The simple sequence listed above was extremely important in the case of *The State of Alaska* v. *Larry Gentry*, tried in Anchorage in April of 1986.

Larry Gentry was a working-class man in his mid-thirties who was charged with being an accomplice in the murder of a pilot named Robert Pfeil. Pfeil was shot from a car which it was claimed belonged to Gentry, and the legal issue revolved around whether or not Gentry knew that his car was to be used in the shooting.

The man who was accused of doing the shooting, John Bright, had been a housemate of Gentry before Gentry's marriage the preceding August. Bright knew how to repair cars and Gentry let Bright use his 1974 Lincoln Continental whenever he wanted it in return for keeping it in running condition. The ignition was wired so that no key was needed to start the car.

While Gentry and his bride were honeymooning in Hawaii, someone was seen in a section of Anchorage shooting a gun at houses or trees, and so Gentry's sister, who was on the Anchorage police force, urged Gentry to get rid of his car, fearing that Bright may have used the car on that occasion.

Gentry had worked at many jobs in Anchorage but his current one was as a bartender at the Fancy Moose, an establishment run by Gilbert (Junior) Pauoli. On several occasions, Pauoli had talked to Bright about "doing a job" for him. On one or two occasions, Gentry was present during these discussions, although Gentry claimed that he never knew what "the job" actually was.

Then, on October 12, 1985, Pfeil was shot. The crime was still under investigation when, on October 29, Gentry went to the police to complain about being harassed by an unknown young man who came to his house and claimed to be the driver in the shooting. The man claimed to be Bright's partner and was still owed $700 for his role in the murder. Since Bright had left town, the man came to Gentry for payment.

During the process of Gentry's questioning by the officers who heard his complaint, Gentry expressed his fear for his life, described what he knew about John Bright and told the police that he had scrapped his Continental because it stopped running. What Gentry did not know was that the young man who wanted his $700 was actually sent to Gentry by the police in an effort to determine Gentry's involvement. One of the officers finally tells Gentry:

> It's sorta strange, John disappears, this guy says he was directly involved and your car suddenly gets crushed. Ya know, that struck me as odd, ya know, apparently from the time you're giving us, it apparently got crushed right after this shooting.

The officers probe a bit further, then Gentry leaves. Four days later, Gentry is back at the police department and he admits to "not being totally up front" with the police about what he knew. Gentry then made statements which, taken together with the testimony of three former employees of Pauoli, appeared to undermine Pauoli's credibility as a witness.

Gentry's second meeting with the police lasted 51 minutes and nine seconds. Gentry attempts, over and over again, to describe how much he feared for his life once he knew what had actually happened. He described how Pauoli said that anyone who told on them would be killed and that Pauoli told him that since he had destroyed the car, Gentry himself was "in it up to his ears."

The police ignore Gentry's expressions of fear, however, and probe for the facts in the case, trying to determine exactly what Gentry knew prior to the shooting itself. Gentry remains firm that all he knew was that Pauoli wanted Bright to do a "job" for him and that it was only after the shooting that he finally knew what had been going on. At the end of the questioning, the police ask Gentry if he would be willing to cooperate with them to catch Bright and Pauoli who are still at large. Gentry heartily agrees to do so and the tape recorder is shut off.

Shortly after the end of this interview, with no tape recorder going, the police ask Gentry to wear a body recorder in any future conversations with Bright or Pauoli. Gentry agrees to this but Alaska State law requires that such a procedure come before a judge in what is called an application for sealed search warrant. That same afternoon of November 2, 1985, Steven Branchflower, from the district attorney's office appears before the Honorable David C. Stewart in such a hearing. Branchflower had apparently heard some of the last minutes of the earlier police investigation and was briefed on the parts he had missed.

It is unclear exactly what Gentry was told by the police or by Branchflower in the interim, but what happened in the ensuing hearing became a nightmare for Larry Gentry. It is clear from the police questioning that Gentry had admitted to buying and selling small quantities of cocaine. It is also clear that he had admitted to aiding in the destruction of what was thought to be evidence in the murder case, his 1974 Lincoln. At issue, however, was his foreknowledge of the shooting or his assistance in it.

Before Gentry entered the hearing room, Branchflower presented his request for authorization for electronic monitoring and recording. At one point, he says:

> The record should show that Larry Ray Gentry is not in the courtroom. He's outside the courtroom with Investigator Austin. And for the court's information, he is not under arrest, he has not been charged. He was called this morning, the testimony will be, and he voluntarily came down to the police station, has given the police a tape recorded confession to his involvement in the matter.

Branchflower's first witness was Officer Michael Grimes, who attempted to recount for Judge Stewart what Gentry had told him. At one point Grimes said: "Gentry still states that he had no idea who it was they – although shooting somebody had been mentioned, he had no idea who it was that John Bright was going to shoot." These words were not an accurate recounting of what Gentry had said on record. Gentry had not admitted to knowing that "the job" was a shooting at all. Grimes continues: "John Bright told Gentry that he was going to use his car and wanted

to use his shotgun ... to do this job. And there was specific
mention of shooting somebody." Again, Officer Grimes evidenced
faulty memory: "It is to me that Gentry stated that Bright had
wanted to use his shotgun which was not the murder weapon,
but Gentry had made no statement about Bright wanting to use
his car and no specific mention of shooting someone."

By this time, Judge Stewart was convinced that Gentry had
indeed confessed to his role in the murder: "I guess what I'm
getting at is I wonder if you could just comment to the voluntari-
ness of his confession to you."

Finally, Gentry is called as a witness. The government had now
claimed that Gentry had admitted foreknowledge of the murder
and the judge had even referred to it as a confession. Or had he?
Branchflower had said only that Gentry had given "a confession
to his involvement." Judge Stewart referred only to "his confession." Certainly Gentry had confessed to his drug dealing and
his attempted destruction of evidence. So in that respect, Branchflower and Stewart were not in error. An admission most clearly
had been made, but not the admission of foreknowledge or assistance in the crime itself. Only Officer Grimes appeared to be confused about this fact, and even a casual inspection of the tape
recording or transcript of that police interrogation could have
made this perfectly clear.

Justice often grinds on without the benefit of available information, however, and since this was a hearing to authorize
electronic monitoring and recording, and since Gentry had not
been charged with any crime, he was not represented by counsel
and, of course, he was not even in the hearing room to hear
Grimes's mistaken representation of the preceding interrogation.

Branchflower's line of questioning of Gentry went straight to
the point of his guilt. Outsiders to the system of justice may find
it odd that a man who has gone to the police voluntarily, admittedly fearful for his life, ignorant of the consequences of his
actions, openly trying to help the police capture Bright and Pauoli,
without legal counsel or advice, could, in the process, become
charged with first-degree murder.

For one thing, Gentry was in a very peculiar position. Being
told that his testimony would help the police obtain the authorization for electronic monitoring and recording, Gentry entered
the hearing with the understanding that he was on the side of

the police. In his own mind, he had admitted nothing more than minor drug dealing and to being directed to destroy his car under threat of his own possible death if he disobeyed. Having admitted this, he could certainly expect to have to pay the consequences. It would behove him, in such circumstances, to appear to be as knowledgeable as possible in order to help convince the judge to grant the authorization. His right to remain silent and his right to have legal counsel were not available to him since he had not been arrested. These rights are called Miranda rights, referring to the 1966 case of *The State of Arizona* v. *Miranda*, which mandated that warnings of constitutional rights are a prerequisite to the interrogation of a subject. Whether it should have been or not, Miranda was not in force. The oddness is that Gentry was in an impossible position: he needed to be truthful; he needed to be convincing; and he needed all the points he could get by being cooperative since he had admitted his drug involvement. What he did not know was that his cooperativeness would be used against him, that the facts of his police interrogation had been misrepresented by Grimes to the assistant district attorney and to the judge.

One might ask, "What difference could this make as long as Gentry told the truth?" The answer is in the analysis that follows. Part of the answer is in the different meanings that the prosecutor and Gentry had for specific words. Part of the answer is in the confusion that both Gentry and Branchflower experienced in getting straight the time frames being discussed. Part of the answer is in the totally different "schemas" or frames of reference that Branchflower and Gentry held. Part of the answer lies in the different speech styles of the two men.

Gentry was, indeed, indicted and brought to trial. His attorney, Mitchell Shapira, called me to analyze the tape-recorded police interrogations and the authorization hearing. I did so and then testified in Anchorage before Judge Mary Green. The prosecution objected strenuously to the admission of my testimony but, after *voir dire*, Judge Green ruled that I indeed had specialized knowledge that would be beneficial to the jury, that the techniques presented were established in the field of linguistics, that the application of these procedures and techniques to law could be helpful, that the jury would not be confused or misled by the presentation of such analysis and that the offering of such analysis was crucial to the defense theory and probative. Judge Green ruled that even though the evidence was the English language, the issue was not simple and that such testimony would assist the triers of facts.

Words used

My first point concerned the differences in word meanings used by Branchflower and Gentry. This issue gets at the question of how much Larry Gentry knew before the shooting took place. Did he know that "the job" he overheard Pauoli discuss with Bright was indeed a shooting? In his police interrogation, Gentry denied this. At the beginning of the authorization hearing, Officer Grimes affirmed it, despite Gentry's own words to the contrary. Branchflower, who heard little or nothing of the police interrogation, based his attack on Officer Grimes's testimony, as the following portions of the tape make clear. Note the emphasized words.

Branchflower	*Gentry*
But you *knew*, you *knew* it was some sort of shooting, but nothing more specific than that.	
	I *wasn't too sure* on it even being a shooting . . . I *wasn't sure*, but I *kind of knew* and I *kind of didn't know*.
You kind of *suspected* though.	
	Yeah I *suspected* . . . 'cause it was just *bits and pieces* I was hearing and picking up, you know, and *started getting a hold of*.
Now by then you *knew* that it involved a shooting, but you didn't *know* who the guy was.	

Yeah, it went on so long
I just *figured* it wasn't
going to happen. You know,
it was just a bunch of
bullshit.

Was it *clear in your mind*
that this was the money that
Pauoli had promised to pay
John for this shooting?

Now we're still talking
before the shooting, right?

I was *pretty sure* of it, yes.

Right. By the time it was
going to happen, yeah, I
knew about it. *I'd done
figured it out* ... The night
it was going to happen *I'd
done figured it out.*

So you *knew* it was going to
happen?

Yes.

Isn't it true that you *knew*
prior to the shooting, that
John was going to shoot
somebody, although you
didn't know who it was?

Your car was to be used.

Yes, I knew about it. *I'd
done figured it* out.

No *I did not know* he was
going to use that car.

Isn't it true that in your
mind you *realized* that you
were assisting John to do
this shooting?

You didn't want to believe it
but you *knew* what was
going on.

I was still *trying to ignore
it.*

Yeah. *I didn't want to believe* it and I knew it was like a nightmare I couldn't get out of.

Looking back on it now, are you willing to accept responsibility for the fact that *you did knowingly assist* in the shooting?

Well I guess I have to. I'm still *trying to believe* I didn't assist in it.

But you *know* that you did.

That's the *way it looks*, yes.

How does it look to you?

It *looks like* I assisted in it and I *didn't want to*.

The preceding are selections from different parts of the tape, held together by the common theme of what Gentry knew prior to the shooting. Branchflower is dogged in his efforts to get Gentry to admit that he knew that "the job" was to be a shooting. In response to the prosecutor's *knew*, Gentry's words provide an interesting contrast, as follows:

- I wasn't too sure
- I wasn't sure
- I kind of knew and I kind of didn't know
- I suspected
- it was just bits and pieces
- started getting a hold of
- I just figured
- it was a bunch of bullshit
- pretty sure of it
- I'd done figured it out
- I'd done figured it out
- I'd done figured it out
- trying to ignore it
- didn't want to believe it
- trying to believe I didn't assist
- I didn't want to

At issue here is what it means to *know* something. When a person knows something, three steps are followed:

1 One believes it to be true.
2 One has good reason to believe it to be true.
3 There is a substantial probability that it is true.

From Gentry's responses to Branchflower's requests for his knowledge, it is extremely difficult to get beyond step one. It is clear that Gentry does not indicate a substantial probability that he knew that a shooting would take place based on what he heard Bright and Pauoli discuss. It is even difficult to determine that Gentry had good reason to believe it to be true. What Gentry admits is suspecting it to be true from the bits and pieces that he was starting to get hold of and figure out. We might ask what it means to have "done figured it out." The verb, to figure, has its origins in mathematics and refers to the process of computation, not to the answers. Nor does it imply accuracy or correctness. It is analogous to the expression, "I calculate he'll be here tonight," where one could substitute the verb *figure* for *calculate* and achieve a similar meaning.

It is equally interesting to notice that even when Gentry appears to agree with Branchflower's use of *knew* he then goes on to modify it to *figured out* or *pretty* sure (not certain). Gentry's testimony in this authorization hearing was consistent with what he said about his lack of foreknowledge of the shooting in the two police interviews that preceded it. In light of this, Branchflower's constant probing on this issue seems odd, until we realize that his efforts were prompted by the mis-statement of Gentry's testimony by Officer Grimes. A mistaken fact, once created, is difficult to get rid of, even for a well-intentioned prosecutor.

Schemas

The second major point my testimony addressed was the difference in schemas, or frames of reference, held by Branchflower and Gentry in this hearing. A person's schema is essentially the way he or she looks at things. The concept of schema, used first by Kant, became an important construct for the psychological study of memory beginning in the 1930s, although it is universally understood that two people will see different things in the same event.

In conversations or interviews, a person's schema can be discovered by the topics they introduce or return to. In this hearing, it is clear that Gentry has two major schemas: to express his fear for his life and to cooperate in any way he can. He repeats these themes over and over again. From the very outset of the hearing, Gentry repeats the schema of fear that he stressed in his earlier interrogation by Officers Grimes and Austin.

What is fascinating about both interviews is that almost every time Gentry brings up how scared he is, the interviewers not only fail to respond to it but also change the subject to something completely different. The one time Branchflower responds to Gentry's expression of fear, he misunderstands the fear as being afraid of testifying in a courtroom. This is not what Gentry was saying. On 13 occasions in the hearing, Gentry describes his fear for his life. On five more occasions, Gentry points out how either Pauoli or Bright have indicated that anyone who "finks on them" will be killed. In four of these incidents, Gentry indicates that he had been thinking about going to the police but was too scared to do so because of their threats. Not once were Gentry's statements responded to by Branchflower, who had his own quite different schemas. Gentry's other schema was to cooperate with the police to capture Bright and Pauoli. He repeats this message 13 times in the hearing alone.

Branchflower's schemas were clearly stated as well. For one thing, he wanted to get the authorization for electronic monitoring and recording. Secondly, Branchflower wanted to get Gentry to admit under oath what Officer Grimes had indicated he confessed in the preceding police interrogation. Thirdly, in all fairness to the prosecutor, Branchflower attempted to confirm what he believed to have happened concerning the shooting.

When placed in juxtaposition, these different sets of schema reveal an interview which is, by definition, at cross purposes:

Gentry's schemas	*Branchflower's schemas*
Fear for my life	Get authorization
Cooperate with police	Get Gentry to admit foreknowledge
	Confirm what I believe happened

In interviews, as in conversation, shared agendas, at least on some points, are a necessary requisite for communication. When there is no shared agenda, miscommunication is extremely likely.

Conversational style

But schema differences were not the only factor to cause Judge Green to consider this hearing complex enough to require expert assistance. The conversational styles of the two participants were equally asymmetrical.

Conversational style is basically the way meaning is communicated in ways other than through individual words by themselves. Linguists call this social meaning, as opposed to word meaning. Another way to think of style in language is to consider it the way of speaking that characterizes a specific person. It is something like a person's fingerprints or written signature. One interesting paradox of language is that, when we use it, we need to be enough alike each other to be understood but, at the same time, different enough from each other to express our individuality or uniqueness.

We do not necessarily develop our style with any conscious effort but these styles emerge, nonetheless, in the ways we walk, write, gesture, and talk, among other things. Since styles are patterned, that is, they occur over and over again, in much the same ways, they can be studied, described, and analyzed as part of a person's identity. Since styles of language are important ways of communicating meaning in conversation, they should not be overlooked as influences on the way understandings develop or misunderstandings occur.

Articulate and competent speakers learn to be careful to develop styles which do not lead to interference with the meaning they wish to convey. Less competent speakers tend to have a great deal of difficulty, especially when talking with more competent speakers. Larry Gentry was not a competent or articulate speaker. Although high school educated, his ability to narrate, describe, and make points clearly and efficiently was sadly lacking. Assistant District Attorney Branchflower, by contrast, was used to public discourse, trained in law and was a clearly competent speaker.

Time referencing   One critical aspect of an interview about what happened in the past is the ability of the narrator to keep time references clear. Unless this is done, the listener can become very confused. Branchflower tried valiantly to set up three time frames for Gentry to work within: what happened prior to the shooting, what happened on the day of the shooting and what happened after the shooting. Gentry was asked to approach these time frames in sequence and not to mix them up. Despite his efforts, Branchflower had considerable difficulty in keeping these three time frames separate. A simple plotting of how the time reference shifted back and forth reveals this difficulty (figure 5.2). The page references in figure 5.2 are to the specific pages in the hearing transcript.

In a case involving possible foreknowledge of murder, confusion about time referencing, even after the interviewer tried so desperately to keep time periods separate, took on great importance. A competent and articulate speaker might have been able to do this effectively. Gentry did not.

One problem Gentry faced was in describing what happened *prior* to the shooting without using terms or facts that he had learned *after* the shooting. For example:

Gentry: I still don't know who they're talking about.
Branchflower: What was John talking about?
Gentry: He was talking about this *shooting* here.

On at least eight occasions in this interview, Gentry used terms or facts that he had otherwise claimed *not* to have known prior to the shooting to describe what occurred. In the above passage, Gentry called "the job" a shooting, even though he explicitly says over and over again that he did not know that the job was to be a shooting until after it had happened.

The result of Gentry's referencing style was to appear to be inconsistent. The assistant district attorney began to have difficulty with Gentry's representation of past events and his knowledge of them, as follows:

Branchflower: What did John tell you?
Gentry: John said he had a guy that was driving the car.
                   He never told me the name or nothing.
Branchflower: He was going to drive the car?

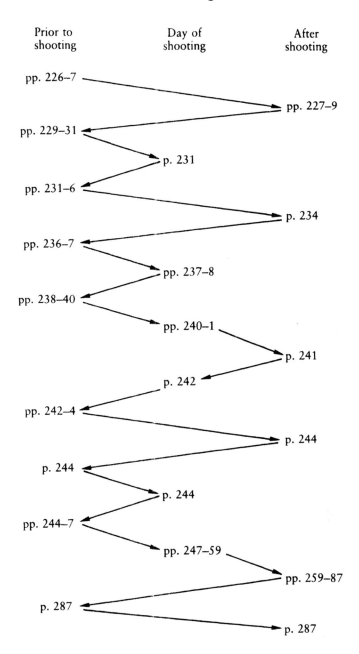

Figure 5.2 Time reference shifts in questioning of Gentry by Blanchflower. (Page references refer to the specific pages of the hearing transcript.)

Gentry:	This was after the shooting.
Branchflower:	Okay.
Gentry:	I didn't even know John was even driving my car to do the shooting.

Here Branchflower is confused by Gentry's verb tenses, especially "was driving," which Branchflower takes to indicate the future. When Branchflower asks, "He was *going* to drive the car?," he is once again trying to determine whether Gentry's knowledge of the crime existed before the shooting took place. Fortunately for Gentry, he caught on to Branchflower's misperception this time and straightened it out before further damage was done. But on many other occasions he did not, leaving the impression that his references to "the shooting" and the murdered man, Robert Pfeil, referred to his knowledge before the shooting, not afterwards.

Slow uptake   Another recurring style of Gentry was to be very slow on the uptake. He tended to respond to a question before thinking it out clearly, again giving the impression of inconsistency. The following examples illustrate this.

Branchflower:	Did they make any promises at all? (*referring to the police*)
Gentry:	No.
Branchflower:	Okay, so you understand –
Gentry:	The only thing they promised was police protection.
Branchflower:	So far you're talking about conversations that happened about two weeks before the shooting.
Gentry:	Yeah.
Branchflower:	Am I right or not?
Gentry:	No. The payment deal happened after the shooting.

Softening   The assistant district attorney also had an identifiable conversational style, a way of talking that re-occurred throughout the interview and shed light on the social meaning of his words. One of these stylistic strategies was to soften the harshness with mitigating modifiers, as follows:

• there came a time this year that you *sort of* got involved in some drugs because of Mr Pauoli?

- there developed a problem in your *sort of* drug dealing here between you and Pauoli, correct?
- We *sort of* have to let the judge decide. We have to let this prosecution *sort of* unwind.

The effect of mitigators such as *sort of*, *kind of*, or *basically* is to soften the blow of the words being used or the charges being made so that an agreeable response might follow and so that the interviewee will not become defensive and clam up completely. A less favorable interpretation of such a style might be that it lulls the respondent or pressures him into agreement.

Multiple questions   In all areas of life where interviewing is done, there is a general understanding that questions should be asked one at a time. Research in doctor–patient interviews and in teacher–student questioning has revealed that when two or more questions are asked at the same time, the respondent answers only the last one in the series. Linguists refer to this as the *recency principle*.

In most areas of life, the use of multiple questioning leads to misunderstanding or omitted facts. In a case of law, such as this one, the stakes are even higher. Branchflower's multiple questions cause Gentry to follow the recency principle but the effect gives the impression that his answer is to *both* questions, not just the last or most recent one, as follows:

Branchflower: Now by then you knew that it involved a shoot-
                  ing but you didn't know who the guy was?
Gentry: Yeah.

Gentry had previously indicated that he didn't know who "the job" was to involve or even what "the job" was. Now Branch-flower, consciously or not, asks two questions at once, the first contradicting Gentry's earlier statement and the second agreeing with it. Gentry follows the recency principle and unknowingly buys into Branchflower's first proposition as well. An articulate, careful, competent speaker might not have been trapped in this way.

In most of life, we do not need to be concerned about such things. Conversation is by definition cooperative. Otherwise there would be no conversation at all. But Gentry was not in a co-operative conversation. He had never been in court before and there was no way that he might know that this interview was adversarial rather than cooperative. His schema, as evidenced by his own words and topics, was to cooperate with the police by helping them capture Bright and Pauoli. He was told that this hearing was to obtain authorization from the judge for Gentry to wear a body microphone and to get the two suspects' words on tape. Gentry's schema was one of cooperation. It is difficult enough for most people to deliberately bypass their natural inclination to respond only to the last, most recent question in a series. But with a schema of cooperativeness in addition, Gentry had little chance here. It looked as if he was saying yes to both of Branch-flower's questions.

There are several instances of Branchflower's style of multiple questioning in this hearing, but the most damaging to Gentry was the following:

> *Branchflower*: Isn't it true that you knew, prior to the shooting, that John was going to do the shooting, that John was going to shoot somebody, although you didn't know who it was?
>
> *Gentry*: Yes.
>
> *Branchflower*: Your car was to be used.
>
> *Gentry*: No I did not know he was going to use that car.

It appeared to the prosecution that Gentry was agreeing to his prior knowledge that a shooting was going to take place and that John Bright was going to do it. Branchflower's three questions ended with the one least harmful to Gentry and it is most likely that Gentry's "yes" was to it, following the recency principle. A stronger conversationalist might have attended better to all three questions and denied the first two before agreeing to the third. Gentry was not that strong.

Changing Gentry's words Assistant Attorney General Branch-flower also slipped into the style of inaccurately repeating the words Gentry had previously used. For example, on p. 241 of the hearing transcript, Gentry had said the following: "I didn't even know John was even driving my car." Then on the next page

Branchflower asks: "When did he take your car? When did you *give* him your car?" Again, on p. 242, Gentry said: "I think he [John Bright] came in the house once and left real quick." On the very next page Branchflower attempts a restatement of Gentry's words as follows:

Branchflower: That day when John picked up your car, I think you said it was two days before, he ran in and said "I'm looking for this guy and I've got your car." You knew, didn't you, that he was going to use your car to –
Gentry: No I did not. I did not know he was going to use my car to shoot this guy out of. I had no idea he was going to do that.

In this case, Branchflower parlays Gentry's "came in the house once and left real quick" into a direct quotation which Gentry had never said and to a meaning which Gentry had never produced.

The affect of the differences in words used, the differences in schemas and the differences in conversational styles made for great confusion in this hearing. The government believed that Gentry had admitted to knowingly assisting in the murder and charged him with first-degree murder. The defense claimed that Gentry admitted to drug involvement and to assisting (under great pressure) in the destruction of material evidence, his old Lincoln. Despite the linguistic evidence noted above, the jury deliberated briefly and found Gentry guilty as charged.

7

Telling the Truth versus Perjury

When a witness is sworn in court, he or she agrees that what is said will be the truth, the whole truth and nothing but the truth. This sounds simple enough. Something is either true or not true, we reason. But things are never that simple.

Courtroom strategy, whether for the prosecution or the defense, causes truth to be more elusive than it would otherwise appear. For example, an attorney may ask a witness, "Were you on medication and seeking a physician's opinion?" If the witness was on medication but not seeking a doctor's assistance, there is no way to answer with either a *yes* or a *no*. Some attorneys under some circumstances permit the witness to explain that their answer is partly *yes* and partly *no*. Some attorneys in some circumstances will permit no explanation and will instruct the witness to answer with either a yes *or* a no, but not both. In such cases, there is no way that the truth can be produced by witnesses. They may want to tell the whole truth and nothing but the truth but they are prevented from doing so by the very process that demands it.

Most witnesses are not skilled enough verbally to match attorneys who are practiced in winning their cases. They are not aware that in every question they are asked, a possible trap is lurking. For example, Prosecutor Jack Strickland in *The State of Texas* v. *T. Cullen Davis* asked me the following question in my cross-examination in that case: "Dr Shuy, when you did this subjective analysis of these tape recordings, what type of tape recorder did you use?" My first reaction was to respond to the main clause in this sentence and tell him that I had used a Bang and Olufsen Beocord 8000. But I had been well warned by one of the attorneys in this case, Sam Guiberson, that such questions might be asked.

"Listen carefully to each part of every question," he warned me. If I had followed my natural inclination to respond to the main clause, I would have "bought into" the subordinate clause as well. I would have essentially agreed that my analysis was subjective, not objective. Strickland would then have been able to characterize my analysis as opinionated, highly interpretive and unreliable. Fortunately, Guiberson's advice was fresh in my mind when the question was asked and I responded that I did not consider my analysis to be subjective but that I had used a Bang and Olufsen machine.

The reporting of facts is probably the most frequent speech act uttered. When the facts are reported accurately, truth is said to have occurred. When the true facts are not known by the listeners, it becomes more difficult to tell whether or not the speaker has spoken truthfully. In such cases, the major evaluation tool for determining truth is that of consistency. That is, if a person says one thing one time and a different thing at another time, one of the two utterances is likely to be untrue. When this happens, the speaker may be charged with perjury, or lying. Likewise, if an attorney requests, suggests, or even implies to clients that they should not tell the truth, that attorney can be charged with suborning perjury. Both perjury and suborning (encouraging) perjury are subject to criminal indictment and trial. This chapter describes one case in which a man was charged with untruthfulness in this regard, and another case in which an attorney was charged with encouraging his clients to lie.

Did Steven Suyat perjure himself?

In July 1983, Steven Suyat was indicted by a Federal grand jury and charged with seven counts of perjury. This case was one of a series of indictments that began with what seemed to be a rather typical and innocuous labor dispute. Suyat was the business representative for the Hawaii Carpenters Union on the island of Maui.

In early 1981, the union and C & W Construction, a non-union general contractor, were at odds over the contractor's failure to pay its workers at a rate that complied with prevailing area standard wages. When the contractor refused to pay its non-union employees at the union rate, the union conducted an informational picketing at all of the contractor's construction projects. The contractor then filed unfair labor practices charges with the National Labor Relations Board (NLRB) against the union.

The contractor charged that the union's picketing was not done for informational purposes but, rather, as a means of forcing the contractor to sign the union's collective bargaining agreement. In accordance with NLRB procedure, the union had its Maui business agents file affidavits with NLRB which set forth their position. The unfair labor practices were never litigated, however, since the matter was settled prior to the hearing.

In August 1982, some 18 months later, the US Attorney's Office began a grand jury investigation of alleged perjury by the Maui business agents regarding the statements they made in their NLRB affidavits. At the close of the investigation, indictments were returned against William Nishibayashi and Ralph Torres, two agents who worked with Suyat on Maui. The charges against these two men alleged that the statements they made in their affidavits about their picketing for informational purposes were false. The contractor who was picketed had secretly tape recorded conversations between himself and the two men which he alleged showed that the union's intent was to organize the contractor, rather than to simply inform the public. Both men were convicted at their first trial.

Throughout all this, Suyat was not charged for anything that related to the charges against his fellow business agents. Nevertheless, Suyat was called by the government as a witness in these trials. This surprised Suyat considerably, since he had already appeared before the grand jury on four separate occasions during this investigation and was not indicted. Even more surprising was the fact that the prosecution had no reason to believe that anything Suyat might have to say in his testimony would do anything except hurt the government's case.

It is possible that the prosecution hoped that by calling Suyat as a witness he might make statements which could later be used to base perjury charges against him. At trial, the prosecutor put questions to Suyat that later provided the basis for these charges. Although the government was not able to obtain mis-statements from Suyat on any of the major issues, it had to settle for what appear to be false statements on very minor issues.

Of the seven charges in Suyat's indictment, four of them concern Suyat's statement that he did not know what the term, "organizing" meant. In two charges, Suyat is charged with saying that he did not know the meaning of the term, "scab." In the last count, he is charged with testifying at one point that he remembered some of what a certain person had said in a conversation while some three hours later he testified that he could not recall any of the substance of that conversation. Those who are not familiar with the way indictments are made may find it odd that four separate charges can be made for essentially the same thing, namely saying that he did not know the meaning of the term, "organizing." But this is common practice in criminal indictments, even though other perspectives may deem it to be four examples of the same thing. The same thing, of course, applies to the two charges in which Suyat claimed not to know how to define "scab."

In a technical sense, each of Suyat's statements may not be true. It is indeed unlikely that a union business agent would not know what the term "organizing" or "scab" means. It is also technically true that persons should be consistent in what they remember of a given event. As is always the case, however, these seven charges must be examined in the context in which they occurred. The indictments may be believable and convincing outside such a context, but they were not uttered outside of context.

Context, to a linguist, means two things: the linguistic context and the social context. The *linguistic context* is simply what words and sentences occurred before and after Suyat's responses. The *social context* includes the non-language factors surrounding the statements: the place where the event took place, the social status and education of the participants, the conversational routine in which the answer was made and other background indicators. Suyat, for example, is a second generation Filipino, born and raised on the island of Molokai. Molokai is a very small island with a population of approximately 12,000 people. It can be described as a "backwater" area. The island has one high school which graduates fewer than 100 students each year. Most of the inhabitants of Molokai work in the cane fields or factories, since Molokai is one of the last of the sugar plantation towns in the state. Suyat is a Molokai high school graduate who went on to technical school and learned a trade. After seven years as a carpenter, he was offered a position with the union as a business agent.

The language context of Suyat's words must be seen in relation to this social context. Many people in Hawaii, especially those from what is called "the neighbor islands," speak a kind of "pidgin" English in their everyday daily dealings with each other. The structure of this form of English is quite different from standard English, both in form and in discourse routines. It seldom happens that speakers of Hawaiian pidgin English find themselves in situations where the standard forms are required. Even in his work on Maui, Suyat was often surrounded by pidgin speakers and he never really mastered the forms of the language required in a formal court setting.

This difference between his everyday language ability and what was required in a court of law was quite apparent to Suyat. He was, of course, nervous and afraid when he was called by the government as a witness in the trial of his two fellow business agents.

Counts one through four of Suyat's indictment concerned his denial that his job was to organize. But the passages from Suyat's testimony that served as a basis for these charges are quite instructive.

Count 1
Prosecutor: And one of the jobs of the business agent is to organize non-union contractors, is that right?
Suyat: No.

Count 2
Prosecutor: So no part of your job is to organize contractors?
Suyat: No.

Count 3
Prosecutor: And so no part of Mr Nishibayashi's job is to organize contractors?
Suyat: That's right.

Count 4
Prosecutor: And no part of Mr Torres' job is to organize contractors?
Suyat: That's right.

From the above four responses, it is clear that Suyat believed that his job, and the job of any other union business agent, was *not* to organize contractors. But the question is, "What did Suyat believe the prosecutor was asking him?" To the average reader, it may or may not be clear that when the prosecutor said "organize contractors" he meant "organize contracting companies" or "organize the workers in contracting companies." But to a man who was trying hard to state the actual fact, the words could mean something quite different. Indeed, most dictionaries define "contractor" as the person who contracts to perform work or to provide supplies. In Suyat's mind at least, "contractor" meant just this. He responds, in essence, that union business agents do not organize the people who negotiate contracts or get them to join the union. Such people are usually owners or management and are not proper subjects for unionization. "Do the unions organize owners?" "Of course not, they organize workers."

Suyat is not an eloquent speaker of English. The preceding interpretation of what he perceived the prosecutor meant by "organized contractors" is as good as the government's interpretation. Any given listener may interpret the prosecutor's words in either way. There is one more bit of evidence, however, which supports our interpretation of Suyat's perception. It occurs shortly after the four quotations which form the basis for his first four charges:

> *Prosecutor:* Now I'll ask my question again, given the fact that this is Mr Nishibayashi's logbook, and given your prior testimony, is this statement: Gave Ralph and Steve more time for organizing non-union contractors and visiting job sites. Is that, according to your prior testimony a false statement?
>
> *Suyat:* According to what he wrote in here is depends how he put it in words.
>
> *Prosecutor:* I'm asking you, is it true or false?
>
> *Suyat:* It's false.

The prosecutor by now had introduced Nishibayashi's logbook in which Nishibayashi actually used the same expression, "organizing non-union contractors." His theory was, if Nishibayashi used these words, why wouldn't Suyat understand them? Suyat's response was typically inelegant. He is saying, in effect, that this was an odd way of saying it but it's still not true that business agents organize contractors. Oddly enough, this passage was not used by the prosecution as a count against Suyat, even though his answer was consistent with the preceding four questions.

Counts five and six concern Suyat's knowledge of the meaning of the word, "scab." Again, the perjury charge is based on Suyat's testimony in the trial of his two colleagues:

Count 5
Prosecutor: What does the word "scab" mean?
Suyat: I have no recollection.

Count 6
Prosecutor: You don't know what the word "scab" means?
Suyat: No.

When a person is asked for the meaning of a word, there are several levels of understanding possible:

1 A dictionary definition.
2 A personal definition.
3 Someone else's personal definition.

It is common practice, when we ask questions, to try to indicate exactly what type of response we want. From the prosecutor's questions, it is clear that a global, dictionary definition is requested. The standard question-asking style to elicit a personal definition is to ask: "What does the word "scab" mean *to you?*" If the prosecutor was after a personal definition, he could have requested it in the normal way.

It is instructive, now, to examine the passage of Suyat's testimony in which this alleged perjury takes place:

Prosecutor: What does the word "scab" mean?
Suyat: Pardon?
Prosecutor: What does the word "scab" mean?
Suyat: I have no recollection.
Prosecutor: You don't know what the word "scab" means?
Suyat: No.
Prosecutor: So you don't remember what you meant by it when you put it down here?

Suyat: Well, yeah.
Prosecutor: Thank you. I have no further questions your honor.

Since the prosecutor gave Suyat no indication that he wanted
Suyat's personal definition, Suyat declined to give a dictionary
definition. Being relatively uneducated and trying to be as accurate as possible, Suyat admits to having "no recollection" of
the proper definition of the word. Now the prosecutor changes
his question strategy and includes the words "what you meant
by it." For the first time, it is clear that a personal definition is
requested. To this, Suyat responds, "Well, yeah."
   The meaning of this last exchange cannot be passed over lightly,
as the prosecutor did. Linguists often speak of "concord rules"
in English questions. This means that if a question is asked
positively (without negatives such as *not*), an answer which is
affirmative must be stated with positives. On the other hand, a
question that is asked using negatives is answered affirmatively
with negatives. This simply means that the responder agrees with
the proposition of the question by using negatives in answer. For
example, if a person asks "But that never happened, did it," and
the respondent says "No," the response is affirmation of the
negativity in the question. The respondent is actually saying "I
agree, it never happened." This is called negative concord. We
agree by using negatives, just as the question did. All native
speakers of English do this intuitively, without conscious knowledge of following a rule.
   In fact, Suyat had used negative concord accurately in other
parts of his testimony and the prosecutor gave no indication of
misunderstanding it:

Prosecutor: But that *never* happened with regard to supplies or
                anything? He *never* wanted to put up the picket line
                just to stop supplies from coming in?
Suyat: No, *no, no.*

In this exchange, the prosecutor used negatives in his question,
and therefore, in order to agree with the proposition, Suyat
affirms it with a negative response or negative concord.
   In another instance, the prosecutor used an even more complex
construction in his negative question:

> *Prosecutor*: And since this says that you and Ralph talked to Mr Jaynes, this is not inconsistent with your previous testimony?
>
> *Suyat*: Yes.

Here Suyat manages to wade through a grammatically acceptable double negative, which produces a positive effect in which the question really asks, "Is this consistent with your previous testimony?" Suyat's affirmation "yes," indicates that he believes it to be not inconsistent with his previous testimony. In this exchange, Suyat translated the two negatives into a positive and responded with positive concord.

There were, in this testimony, additional exchanges indicating that Suyat was able to handle both positive and negative concord. Thus, when the prosecutor ended his direct examination with a negative question, "So you *don't* remember what you meant by it when you put it down there," Suyat's response, "Well, yeah" indicates that he indeed *did* remember what *he* meant. Up until now, however, he understood the prosecutor's question to be: "Can you give me a dictionary definition of 'scab'," to which the answer is "No." Now the question is changed to "What do *you* mean by 'scab'?" Suyat is saying, in effect, "Yes I remember what I meant by it," but he never got a chance to define it because the prosecutor quickly ended his examination with "No further questions."

In most of life's conversations, a person in Suyat's position could then say, "Wait a minute. I haven't had a chance to tell you what I meant by 'scab.'" The courtroom is not a place where such an emendation can be made, however. Witnesses can only answer questions that have been asked. They cannot volunteer new topics or start new question/answer sequences. Once cut off, they must be quiet. Once misunderstood, they must live with the misunderstanding. Discourse rules are discourse rules and unless the witness's attorney deems the misunderstanding important enough to recycle in his cross-examination, it remains a misunderstanding.

Apparently the defense attorney never caught on to the significance of this muddle, for he did not bring it up on cross-examination. At any rate, the odd thing about this situation was that Suyat was called as the prosecution's witness and, as such, his plight was of no real concern to any of the attorneys present.

If he happened to incriminate himself during his testimony, he was not the defense attorney's responsibility. In effect, he had no legal counsel in this trial, no one to watch out for his own good. He was the witness of the prosecution and he was incriminated by this circumstance.

Count 7, the last charge on Suyat's indictment for perjury, claimed that what Suyat said at the trial was inconsistent. On direct examination, he had told the prosecutor the following:

Prosecutor:	Do you recall him ever having any conversations with Ralph Torres?
Suyat:	Yes.
Prosecutor:	Do you recall when those were?
Suyat:	No.
Prosecutor:	Do you recall what he said to Ralph Torres?
Suyat:	No.
Prosecutor:	Do you recall what Ralph Torres said to him?
Suyat:	No.

Some three hours later, on cross-examination by the defense, the following exchange occurred:

Defense attorney:	Do you recall what Mr Torres said in response to this?
Suyat:	I believe Mr Torres, I think, told him that he received a letter from Honolulu and everything is respond back to the Honolulu office, to Mr Kupau.

(handwritten margin note: now he recalls?)

There can be no question about the inconsistency of these two exchanges. It is quite another matter, however, to attribute such inconsistency totally to perjury. For one thing, three hours of focus on a topic could have stimulated his memory. In any case, the information that Suyat provided is highly qualified with "I believe" and "I think." In addition, Suyat was likely to be more comfortable with the defense attorney's questions than with the prosecutor's. When a person is afraid of the consequences of being inaccurate in recall, one takes the safer road of "I don't know" or "I can't recall." With the defense attorney, the pressure was not as great.

Throughout his testimony, Suyat made every effort to be as

explicit as possible with the prosecutor. Linguistic evidence of
this effort is abundant in Suyat's responses, as follows:

Requests for clarification	25
Qualifies statements	32
("I believe," "I think," etc.)	
Adds specifics to prosecutor's questions	7
Corrects prosecutor's generality	1

Another clue to why Suyat tried to be more explicit in his
answers to the prosecutor than he was in his answers to the
defense attorney can be found in the verbs the attorneys used to
elicit information about past events. The prosecutor habitually
used the verb, *recall* (16 times) in his direct examination. The
defense attorney used it only five times, more habitually using
remember. To questions using the verb, *recall*, Suyat responds
almost entirely with *no* or with a request for clarification. When
the question containing the verb *recall* contains a qualification,
however, Suyat provides a qualified response, as follows:

> Prosecutor: Do you ever *recall* hearing the contractor in your
> presence saying *anything either* to you *or* anyone else?
> Suyat: I believe, yes.
> (. . .)
> Prosecutor: Do you *recall* him ever having *any* conversations with
> Ralph Torres?
> Suyat: Yes, I think.

It is most likely, based on an analysis of Suyat's responses to
questions posed with the verb *recall* that Suyat inferred that to
recall required a precision of memory and expression that he was
simply unable to provide. If this is the case, it would not be the
only word that the prosecutor defined differently from the humble
young man from the sugar plantation. By then, they had tangled
over the meanings of the following terms:

Word	Prosecutor's definition	Suyat's definition
"friend"	person with whom you socialize after work	work associate

"accurate"	true	specific and/or complete
"check on"	get people to join the union	see how many jobs there were
"make sure"	prevent people from crossing the picket line	find out the times when the workers were working
"approve"	know about or agree with	officially endorse or counter-sign
"caught"	prevent from crossing the picket lines	note the exact times that the pickets are crossed

On a good day, with a little luck and with an attorney to protect him, Steven Suyat might have been able to defend himself in his testimony as the government's hostile witness against his fellow union business agents. The semantic muddle about organizing contractors versus organizing workers might have been untangled to the extent that four of the charges would never have been possible. Likewise, the confusion about the type of definition of "scab" requested by the prosecutor might have been resolved, wiping out two more of the charges. Under happier circumstances, the issue of negative and positive concord could have revealed that Suyat was, in fact, agreeing that he did remember what he meant by the term "scab" but was simply unable to define it in a manner he deemed acceptable in a courtroom filled with learned people.

Finally, the alleged inconsistency in Suyat's recall of a conversation with Torres might have been seen for what it was, a fear of not being explicit enough to the prosecutor to even attempt the broad strokes that he remembered three hours later when the same question was put to him by the defense attorney. But this was not a good day for Steven Suyat. He had no luck at all and, even worse, he was put in the absurd position of being impeached by the very attorney who called him to testify. Worse yet, the defense attorneys were not technically responsible for representing his best interests either. So he was on his own and, as soon as his testimony was over, he was indicted on seven counts of perjury.

As the time of Suyat's own perjury trial approached, his attorney, Mark Kawata called me to help analyze the evidence, presented

above. The judge would not permit the expert witness testimony
that could have clarified these issues. Suyat was convicted on all
six counts.

Did Donald Crow suborn perjury?

In July, 1980, two US postal inspectors entered the office of the
attorney Don Crow of Kansas City and requested that he help
them with a personal injury claim resulting from an automobile
accident. Such events are common to many attorneys and, to
Don Crow at least, this day seemed like any other day and these
clients like many others who came to his office. The difference,
of course, was that they were not the Vernacular Black English
speaking, inner-city, working-class people that they pretended to
be. They were government investigators, part of a large plan to
stop fraudulent personal injury claims in that area. Some of their
work paid off, for several physicians and attorneys were indicted
in this effort. But when they targeted Don Crow's practice, they
made a mistake, one that would prove costly to the government
and come close to financially and emotionally ruining the attorney.
   Like agents of the FBI, the Internal Revenue Service and other
law enforcement agencies, these postal inspectors wore hidden
microphones and tape recorded their conversations with Crow
and anyone else who happened to be within earshot. They also
tape recorded telephone conversations. In all, 17 conversations
were taped.
   Unlike the case of Steven Suyat, the government's effort to discover perjury was not to contrast what was said on one occasion
with what was said at another time. Instead, the technique was
to pretend that they were automobile accident victims (no accident actually had occurred) and to get the attorney to file a claim
based on fraudulent information. During this process, it would
be necessary to let the attorney know that this was, indeed, a
fraudulent claim. Otherwise, there would be little grounds for
charging him with a crime. At issue, then, was whether or not
the agents ever made it clear that their claim was fraudulent.
Along with this is the issue of whether or not the attorney ever
encouraged them to embellish their story, alter the facts or, indeed,

to lie. If it could be shown that he did so, he could be charged with suborning perjury.

As with many scam operations, the agents faced a difficult task. If they were to walk into an attorney's office and declare that they had never really been in an accident but that they were filing a claim just to make a little money, even a dishonest lawyer might back off. For one thing, it might appear to be a set-up to trap the lawyer. In addition, such brashness might cause even an unscrupulous attorney to turn the case down because anybody who acted so openly could not be trusted to keep the charade secret.

The Postal Inspectors Office, therefore, cooked up a different scheme. They selected black agents who were familiar with black working-class culture and language to pose as clients. Whether intentional or not, this decision cleverly aided their effort to be indirect about the non-authentic claims. By feigning inarticulateness and ignorance, they caused the attorney to have to infer what their meaning really was. By not knowing how to talk about what had allegedly happened to them, they drew on the lawyer's ability to piece together a coherent story. If Attorney Crow should happen to infer accurately that their case was bogus and if he subsequently went along with their charade, he would be guilty of encouraging them to lie.

This scheme had much in common with the one used by the FBI to offer a bribe to Senator Harrison A. Williams Jr (see chapter 2). In that scenario, the agent posed as an Arab sheik and spoke such broken English that the senator actually had to help him utter his thoughts by prompting him in English. Such a situation gives the appearance of collaborating in the illegal act when, in fact, it is nothing more than sympathetic assistance to an inarticulate person, an act of kindness which anyone might do under the same circumstances.

It is necessary, in analyzing conversations between an attorney and a client, to first determine the normal structure of such an exchange. Just as it was necessary to determine the structure of a bribery event in the Clayton case (see chapter 3), it was necessary in Crow's case to discover what a regular interview with a personal injury client might look like. Only then would it be possible to determine whether or not the attorney had strayed from this structure into something more irregular. Analysis of such interviews reveals a six-part structure, as follows:

1 Confirm that the accident occurred.
2 Confirm that medical treatment was received.
3 Confirm that the medical problem has persisted.
4 Prepare a contract and authorization for medical information.
5 Execute the claim.
6 Resolve the claim.

The question then became, "Did Attorney Crow follow this sequence and elicit all aspects of the structure?" Examination of the tape-recorded interviews indicates clearly that he did so.

The agents produced a written police report of the accident and an oral description of their alleged injuries. The agents all reported seeing a specifically named physician for their injuries. They also reported that their injuries were persistent and that they were currently receiving treatment twice a week from that doctor. At this point, Crow prepared a contract and got them to sign authorizations for the release of their medical records. Crow then executed their claims and about six months later resolved theirs claim by presenting them with a check for their injuries. In short, there was nothing irregular about the structure of the procedure. Crow followed the normal pattern and elicited the appropriate information. The government's case could not be made in this area.

The indictment of Crow was made, then, not on the basis of the procedures he followed, but on the way he responded to the words of the agents. While Attorney Crow thought he was interviewing these clients, they were actually interviewing him without his even being aware of it. The two different but concurrent interviews contained totally different agendas, often providing a peculiar dissonance to the conversation. Whereas Crow is trying to obtain the information necessary for him to decide whether or not there is justification for making a claim, the inspectors posing as clients had an agenda of trying to catch the attorney acting illegally.

For example, the inspectors recycle the topic of the doctor's medical report nine times before Crow is ready to talk about it. During this part of the conversations, Crow referred only to the medical authorization forms. In other words, Crow was assuming, on the basis of what the clients told him, that a medical report would be forthcoming. In his own mind, he had moved on to the next step in the process, getting authorization for this medical information to be released. By bringing up the topic of the medical report so often, the inspectors were opening the door for Crow to question the validity of such a report, to catch on to their indirect hints at the illegality of what they were doing, to wink at the process and thereby to incriminate himself. Crow never bites on this. The signals from the inspectors were too indirect. Their role of incoherence and ignorance were all too familiar to the attorney and his work schedule was so crowded that clients moved in and out at a pace far too rapid for him to have time to draw inferences. Crow took them for honest people.

They were not very articulate but they claimed to have the proper support for all aspects of his interview structure. Crow had no reason to believe that they were conning him. He had even less reason to believe that they were actually law enforcement officers.

The inspectors' assumed role of unexpert, inner-city folks also provided another open door for Crow to incriminate himself. Continually they ask Crow to tell them what to do. When a person requests directives of another person, the result is an assignment of power. The requestor is saying, in effect, "I am ignorant and powerless; you tell me what to do because you are knowledgeable and powerful." One of their many requests for directives from Crow was "Do you know a doctor we can go to?" This question was to determine whether or not Crow would send them to one of the physicians already on these inspectors' lists of suspects. The government was trying to discover instances in which doctors and attorneys were consistently collaborating. Crow's response was non-committal and general: "You can go to any doctor you want." Another request for direction is the following: "How many days should I do that work-miss-slip for?" Here the inspector has been told that he needs to get his employer to verify the work days lost because of the accident. The client then asks Crow how many days to write down on the "missed-work-slip." To this, Crow asks, "Did you miss a couple days?" The inspector replies, "Okay," as though Crow's question were actually a directive that he is now agreeing to carry out.

One might ask why the attorney did not try to clarify this misunderstanding about the number of workdays missed. On the other hand, it is common practice for professionals such as physicians, lawyers, or psychiatrists to tolerate the inarticulateness and technical misunderstanding of their clients. The alternative is to correct clients, who are already ill at ease and in a context that they do not comprehend, to teach them the language appropriate to the context, and to correct their misunderstandings of procedures. Neither physicians nor attorneys often take the time to do this. They are paid for their results, not for their instruction. In any case, these clients had already shown great ignorance of both the fields of law and medicine, as the following quotations indicate:

- He is a medicine doctor.
- I was just wanting to let you know in case he sent you any reports.
- I explained to him I needed a report for insurance purposes, so he'd take care of the dates and everything.
- Yeah, they did a report cause he, either he told her upper back and neck and lower back or vice versa.

In each of these cases, Crow could have corrected the clients' misunderstanding of technical terms (such as "medicine doctor") or procedures (such as the need to request release of medical forms before the doctor sends them). Like most professionals, however, he chose to tolerate this inarticulateness or misunderstanding rather than face the difficulty or take time to correct it. By introducing the topic of the doctor's report so many times, the postal inspectors may have inferred that the attorney knew that this was their indirect signal that something illegal was going on. At no point, however, does Crow even respond to their topic. He ignores it and goes on with his systematic line of questioning as though they had said nothing at all.

Thus, two separate contextual understandings emerged. The inspectors may have inferred that Crow understood what they were hinting at. On the other hand, Crow's understanding, as revealed by the language he uses in that context, is that they are inarticulate or ill informed about the process. Crow's questioning strategies throughout these interviews were consistent and clear. He used the same strategies that are used by careful physicians, psychiatrists, police interrogators, newspaper reporters, and other professionals who interview laymen, inarticulate or not:

1 Request for information directly.
2 Recheck information provided.
3 Challenge information provided.
4 Probe for details and information not given.
5 Give advice on how the client can be accurate about the information.

It is the last strategy, giving advice about how to be accurate, that may lead to different inferences about the meaning or knowledge of the attorney. For example, the government claimed that Crow was encouraging the clients to lie in their report of wages lost. The basis of the prosecution's contention was the following passage:

Client: How many days should I, do that work, that miss work slip for, that I got to get?

Attorney: If you only went to the doctor, uh, when did you, when is he [the foreman] going to say that you first went to the doctor?

Client: He's going to say like a couple days after that accident.

Attorney: Okay. The day you went to the doctor, you probably missed that day and the next day.

Client: Okay.

Attorney: So you find out from him [the foreman] what the day is you went to the doctor.

Client: Okie-doke.

The preceding context makes it clear that Crow's reference to "he" is the client's foreman, who must vouch for the fact that he missed work. Since the client is unable to recall what day he went to the doctor, the attorney is advising his client to check with his foreman to determine the first day he missed work since that is, logically, the day he must have gone to the doctor. Unfortunately, the pronoun references of "he" are not explicit in the sentences in which they occur but the larger context gives the indication that "he" refers to the foreman, not to the doctor. This is especially clear in Crow's last statement alone: "So you find out from *him* what the day is you went to the doctor." If Crow had meant "him" to be the doctor, he would have said "find out from the *doctor* what the day is you went to *him*." In this case, the verb "went" is always associated with "the doctor" and the verb "find out" is always associated with the foreman.

To a person not familiar with the case, this whole passage may seem trivial. The client did not recall when he went to the doctor and how many days he missed work. The attorney is simply giving advice about how to find out the facts. The government's contention, however, was that if Crow were telling him to go to the doctor to discover these facts and if the doctor was known or suspected to be crooked, then Crow was in on the scheme to defraud the insurance claim. From the defense point of view, such a charge was pretty doubtful, especially since Crow had not advised the clients which doctor to go to in the first place. In fact, the doctor that they claimed to be using *was* a suspect but the attorney had no way of knowing this at that time. In any case, the government's position was discounted by the contextual analysis of Crow's reference pronoun, *he*. *He* clearly referred to the foreman who had reportedly made out a missed work slip for the client.

The prosecution also made much of the attorney's explanation of the client's rights in a personal injury case. Early in his meetings with the clients, Crow explained: "Okay, let me tell you what it takes to get a recovery from an insurance carrier as a result of a car accident." Crow goes on to explain that the victim has to suffer some kind of injury, that he has to have expended money with the doctor, that if there is no permanent injury then all that can be recovered is wages lost, medical expenses and transportation costs to and from the doctor's office. He went on:

> to get above this, you have to have permanency, continuing aggravation that goes beyond the treatment. In your instances, there is nothing you can recover because you obviously have no permanency. Just because you are in an accident doesn't mean you are entitled to some money.

To this the client responds, "See, everybody else, I guess, must have went to the doctor or something." Crow then says:

> Well, if your injuries or the pain that you suffered reoccurs and you go to a doctor and he administers treatment for that pain and is definitive enough after that treatment to indicate that that pain

will probably occur again and again and again, then you've got a recovery possibility.

In this passage it is quite possible, since the inspectors were carrying out an elicitation interview unknown to the attorney, that they could miss the conditional nature of the attorney's statements. Everything he says is governed by the conditionals *if* and *can*. He explains to the clients that at present they have *no* rights to a claim since they are not suffering pain now and have incurred no medical expenses. But then he explains their future rights: if the pain re-occurs, if they go to a doctor, if he administers treatment, if his diagnosis is definitive enough, etc. It is quite possible that in their effort to see only from the perspective of their own agendas, they simply did not attend to Crow's explanation of their rights based on these conditions and that they inferred that he was telling them what to do, giving a directive instead of giving advice.

The prosecution made much of Crow's explanation of the client's rights and claimed that the attorney was telling them to commit perjury. This interpretation overlooks the context in which the attorney's advice was given, an explanation of their rights, not an encouragement of what to do. The government apparently completely overlooked Crow's use of *if* at the beginning of his statement. English grammar specifies that an initial *if* clause governs all following clauses unless otherwise explicitly changed. Thus, what Crow was saying can be rewritten as follows; with the redundant *ifs* made explicit in parentheses:

> Well, *if* your injuries or the pain that you suffered reoccurs and [if] you go to a doctor and [if] he administers treatment for that pain and [if he] is definitive enough after that treatment to indicate that that pain will probably occur again and again and again, then you've got a recovery possibility.

Crow was not telling the clients what to do. He was simply advising them what their future rights might be, if the conditions specified were met. In any case, the attorney was not suborning perjury.

Crow's attorneys, Pete Smith and Sam Guiberson, called me to assist them in analyzing the surreptitious tape recordings made by the postal inspectors. We went to trial prepared to point out all indications that Crow was not suborning perjury. This testimony was not necessary as the judge, after hearing the prosecution's effort to show guilt, dismissed the case, ruling that the government was not successful in its attempt.

8

Promising

Everybody makes promises. There is nothing unusual or questionable about promises unless the person who makes the promise has no right to do so. For example, if someone were to say, "I promise you that I will give you South America as a birthday gift," the listener might not be very impressed. The speaker does not own South America and has no right to promise it. Such promises are infelicitous because they are impossible. When we make promises, we pledge and commit ourselves to do whatever it is we are talking about. The listener has every reason to believe we will do what we promise and expect to see it accomplished.

People run into trouble about promises for several reasons. If the promiser fails to carry out the promise, the listener can be disappointed or angry. Less obvious, but probably more common in real life, is the difficulty people have with defining and recognizing a promise when it occurs.

The easiest promise to recognize is one in which the verb *promise* actually occurs, as in: "I promise to give you $50." We have already referred to "performative" speech acts, those which perform the action intended with the verb itself. A performative offer, for example, is one in which the speaker says, "I offer you so and so." A performative warning is one in which the speaker uses the verb, *warn*. In this case, a performative promise is one in which the verb *promise* is used explicitly.

There are, however, many other ways to express a promise besides performatively. For example, one might say, "I will give you $50." Such a statement may be intended as a promise, even if the listener may not understand it to be one. Another way to express the same idea might be, "There's $50 in this for you." In this sentence, the agent, "I," is replaced by "There's" and the future aspect expressed earlier by "will give" is made more general and existential with "There's."

As promises are made with expressions farther and farther away from the explicit performative verb, it is less and less clear that a promise was even *intended* by the speaker. In fact, much confusion is likely to take place. The sentence, "I will give you $50," though intended as a promise, may be understood by the listener as a prediction rather than as a promise. That is, it may be perceived as "I predict that at some time in life I will turn $50 over to you." If understood in this way, the speaker's intention of promising is considerably weakened. In the same way, the sentence, "There's $50 in this for you," though intended as a promise, may be understood by the listener as an offer, as in "I offer you $50." Offers, as we have noted earlier, are conditionally based on something in return, as in a business transaction. Promises, on the other hand, are not necessarily associated with such conditions. They can be made out of generosity, or kindness, with nothing expected in return.

Criminal law cases often require the jury to determine whether or not a promise was made. Although there is nothing innately illegal about promising, difficulties may arise when law enforcement agencies believe that a person has promised to do something as a means of getting something in return. In the Abscam case of Senator Williams, the prosecution claimed, for example, that the senator promised to sponsor legislation that would provide immigration for the presumed Arab sheik. If the senator had indeed made such a promise, it would have served as part of the quid pro quo that would show him to be guilty of using his office unlawfully for personal gain.

Did Senator Williams promise to sponsor immigration legislation for the sheik?

The endeavor in all the Abscam cases was to get individual congressmen to agree to sponsor private immigration legislation for the Arab sheik. In return, the sheik would agree to invest his alleged vast wealth in projects beneficial to that congressman's district. Once such an agreement was reached, the FBI's scenario called for the agent to offer the congressman some money, between $20,000 and $50,000, as an out-and-out bribe.

It should be pointed out that there is nothing illegal in sponsoring such legislation. Nor is there anything illegal in the sheik's promise to invest in business ventures in Florida (as in Congressman Richard Kelly's case) or in New York (as in Congressman John Murphy's case). In fact, it is the duty of congressmen to try to develop projects that will benefit the people in their jurisdictions.

Evidence that there is nothing illegal about such a proposition can be demonstrated by the fact that such a promise was made by FBI agent Amoroso to Senator Larry Pressler of South Dakota and the senator was never indicted for it. Pressler's responses were, "My door is open" and "I will research the process." These responses can hardly be interpreted as flat denials. It is also clear from Senator Pressler's words that he did not consider the introduction of special legislation of this type either illegal or untoward:

> There are people who have a, uh, who have introduced special legislation, when, when they keep a maid in the country for a year longer ... I've heard of this and like every, every senator and congressman he's got a, you know, cleaning lady, a maid that he pays less than minimum wages to probably and, a, sometimes they're from a foreign country and their visa runs out and there's a way to introduce a bill. That will delay the machinery ones at the, but that's become so now they're people who check everybody who introduce a special bill and they ask you what your purpose was and so it's not easy to do.

Senator Pressler, in fact, goes on to say, "Most of the people out in South Dakota are mad about foreign investment." By his intonation it is clear that his word "mad" does not mean "angry" but, instead means "anxious to get involved in" or "crazy about." Pressler finally observes that he cannot guarantee anything, at which point agent Amoroso suggests that he is "willing to put out money" and mentions the figure, $50,000. The conversation is interrupted by a telephone call for Amoroso. After the agent returns, he ceases all efforts to conclude the offer of money and urges the senator to think it over. Although it may be said that Senator Pressler did not finally promise to sponsor the legislation, he most certainly did not reject the idea, as his "My door is open" clearly indicates.

In contrast, Representative Michael "Ozzie" Myers from Philadelphia clearly agrees to sponsor such legislation, volunteering such statements as:

- Where I could be of assistance is private bills.
- What ya need is influence.
- We use our influence.
- I'll be in the man's corner a hundred percent.
- We bring him in because he's investing his money here.
- You got my guarantee.

Representative Richard Kelly, in response to Amoroso's request to sponsor private legislation says:

- Let's do it.
- I'm gonna do it.

In contrast to Pressler, who says "My door is open" and to Kelly and Myers, who agree to do it outright, Senator Williams neither agrees to sponsor the legislation nor disagrees. Instead, he points out the many difficulties such legislation might encounter should someone agree to sponsor it:

- It's not easy
- There have to be good reasons
- Meet some criteria
- Harder than it was five years ago
- It has been restricted
- Best results when a person of good character is here
- The situation has to be fully understood
- It's an exceptional situation
- After full knowledge of your situation
- It is processed through a committee ... then also the other body
- Quite frankly I can't issue that
- I cannot personally
- It goes through the whole dignified process of passing a law.

The prosecution in Williams's case claimed that the senator agreed to sponsor this private immigration legislation in return for personal gain. There is grave doubt about what personal gain he might have achieved but, in this case, the issue is whether or not the senator promised to sponsor the legislation at all. From the words he spoke, there is no way to reach such a conclusion.

Nevertheless, the jury reached it. They found him guilty of promising to sponsor the legislation in return for a loan from the sheik to a group of men who wanted to use it to restore an abandoned titanium mine in Virginia. As noted earlier, in this same conversation with the alleged sheik, immediately following was an offer of money: as the shiek put it, "I would like to give you some money for permanent –," Before the sheik could finish his sentence, the senator held up both hands and said "no, no, no, no."

Did Senator Williams promise to put whatever interest he might develop in a blind trust?

Another accusation against Senator Williams was that he promised to *hide* whatever financial interest he might develop in the still-defunct titanium mine. An examination of the senator's own words in the taped conversations reveals that he indeed did make a promise. But the promise he made was not what the prosecution claimed it was:

- I'm going to find a way to protect myself with some kind of *declaration*. I'm going to have to *go public* with something or other.
- We can *blind trust* me, you know.
- There are ways to be *on a certain record*. Now if it's a *blind trust*, that's the way for my purposes.
- Well, there we have it *under the trust*. You see. So I've done what I had to do. But it has to be worked out. It's not easy but it can be worked. I know it can be worked. I know it can be worked.

There is no reason for twisting the senator's words out of context. He is promising to use a blind trust, the procedure required by law of public officials who hold stock during their tenure in office.

Why then was the senator charged with attempting to hide his interest? The answer can only be that those who analyzed these tapes were possibly sloppy or biased in their listening. It is the government agents who utter the terms "hidden interest" on the tapes. When Williams responds with his own solution, his own promise, a blind trust, it is in negative response to the suggestions of illegality offered by the FBI. Why it is that the prosecution, the US Senate Ethics Committee and the jury at his trial could not distinguish between words uttered by the agents and negative reactions to those words uttered by the senator remains a mystery. The charge against Williams was upheld, irrespective of the evidence, in spite of the facts, in spite of the actual language used.

Did Dean Brewer promise to find a pill press?

What happens when someone gives us information that makes us uncomfortable, something that we would rather not hear? Our response options are several but, in reality, we seldom select from among them. Instead, we do what the unwritten but intuitively recognized rules of politeness dictate: we distance ourselves as much as possible, hoping beyond hope that it will all go away and that things will be as they used to be.

In most instances, this unwanted information cannot be wished away. The death of a loved one or friend, a child's bad grade or a famine in Africa are verifiable facts. They will simply not be distanced. But there is another category of reported information that does not seem to be so final, such as when an acquaintance tells us that he or she has committed an illegal act. We would rather not know this and we find it difficult to say anything meaningful. Our focus may turn to "getting through" the conversation and back to more comfortable thoughts. We often resort to formulaic language, offering no topic continuity of our own, or to a heavy reliance on feedback markers such as "uh-huh," "I see," or even less, as in "um."

Such a situation happened to Dean Brewer, owner of a small

company that manufactures chemicals used largely by ink producers, in Atlanta, Georgia in the summer of 1989. The Drug Enforcement Agency had been doing surveillance on a suspect, Bob Slay, very closely, even monitoring his telephone calls. As it turns out, two of these calls were to Brewer, whom Slay had recently met at a barbecue hosted by a mutual friend. After a friendly greeting ritual, Slay says:

> Well, uh, they, they've been working on this stuff for about four days straight ... it's not working too well, not the stuff, just the production of it's not working too well ... and what we're wondering, do you know any, do you have any kinda catalogue or know anybody, or anything that could possibly we could buy a press.

To this Brewer starts to respond, possibly with a request for clarification: "A–." Slay then interrupts Brewer and clarifies: "A pill press." Brewer appears to be surprised. He had recently sold some chemicals to Slay and now he learns that Slay's purpose was to produce pills. Slay later admitted to the police that the pills were mood-altering chemicals of a type commonly called "Ecstasy" (methylenedioxyamphetamine), now illegal.

When Brewer discussed these tapes with his attorney, he did not deny that at this point in the conversation he came to understand what Brewer was making. He claimed that his unspoken reaction at that time was "Oh, my God." Why is it, then, if Brewer learned from this conversation what Slay was really up to, that he did not say something like, "You didn't tell me you were making Ecstasy pills; that's illegal"? In the absence of forthright and explicit expressions of surprise and disappointment, the government alleged that Brewer knew all along what Slay was manufacturing and that he was, himself, a part of the conspiracy. To make matters even worse, Brewer appears to be going along with Slay's request to locate a pill press. After Slay specifies that it is a pill press he is looking for, Brewer says: "Uh, I don't know. I could check around." As Slay continues to describe his predicament of not being able to get the product to stick together properly, Brewer says twice more, "Let me check around," and the first conversation ends.

Eight days later, Slay calls Brewer again. Three times Brewer responds that he has had "no luck," and he suggests: "I wonder if ya'll could use somebody's or something." Again, Brewer had every opportunity to tell Slay that what he was doing was illegal and reprehensible and that he would have nothing to do with the process. He didn't.

On the surface, it would appear that things did not look very good for Dean Brewer, largely because he did not, at the time of the calls, express the appropriate righteous indignation. But such indignation requires more analysis here.

One is reminded of the posturing of certain members of the Senate Ethics Committee during the Committee's hearings on the behavior of Senator Harrison A. Williams Jr, after his Abscam conviction. Over and over again, the Senate Committee commented that "an honest man would have turned his back and walked away" from the bribery offers of the FBI agent posing as an Arab sheik. What actually happened, if the Senate Committee had paid attention to the tape in question, was that the undercover agent posing as a sheik offered Senator Williams $50,000 and the senator replied, "No, no, no, no." The senator tried to point out the necessary procedures for obtaining citizenship for the sheik, all accurate and totally exculpatory, but not full of righteous indignation. Undiscussed in his criminal trial and in the Senate hearings was the simple fact of social politeness required of people in a conversation. The improper words of others are simply not criticized in situations where the speaker, believed to be a foreign diplomat from a country whose canons of behavior may not parallel those of one's own country, deserves to be treated with dignity and respect. Politicians, particularly senators, tend to express a high degree of politeness in all aspects of their behavior. Two senators with diametrically opposed viewpoints will, for example, refer to each other as "the distinguished Senator from the State of –" in public debate. Decorum and politeness prevail.

Even in everyday conversation there are highly recognizable degrees of social politeness. Egregious and utterly inaccurate statements by customers are glossed over by salesmen, whose main goal is not to win an argument but to sell a product. Patients are not impertinent to their physicians. Students are expected to be civil to their teachers and children to respect their parents. Those who succeed in the business world, such as bankers, are politely silent about the obvious gaffes of prospective clients whose investments are critical to the bank's success.

This simple principle is often overlooked in tape cases like the one involving Dean Brewer. He owned a small business which survives only because of customer purchases. Slay was a recent customer who had made what Brewer believed at the time to be a legitimate purchase. But now Slay came back with new information that caused Brewer considerable concern. What should Brewer have done? It is easy for non-involved spectators to say that he should have expressed indignation and walked away. In truth, this is very difficult to do.

So what is it that Brewer actually did? When attorney John Martin asked me to examine the tapes and transcripts in this case I proceeded first with a standard topic analysis, as follows:

Slay		*Brewer*
1		(greeting)
2	Going off for Memorial Day?	
3	They're working on this stuff.	
4	Know anybody who could buy a press?	
5	They're having to do 'em in microwave.	
6	It's not working	
7		Let me check.
8	They're willing to spend a lot.	
9	They worked four days.	
10	They can't get it to form.	
11		Let me check around.
12	I looked in Fisher catalogue	
13	(closing)	

In the second taped telephone conversation:

Slay		*Brewer*
1		(greeting)
2	Have a good Memorial Day?	
3	I went deep sea fishing.	
4	Where did you go?	
5	We gotta get this stuff going.	
6	Press in NY for $75,000.	

7	We're trying to find one around here.	
8		I haven't had any luck.
9	A guy said they wouldn't get them to stay together without chemicals to be pressed	
10		Could you use somebody's?
11	We may have to buy that one.	
12	We're trying to rent it.	
13	Just wondered if you found it.	
14	I'll keep you posted.	
15	We can't get it to stay.	
16	They had it ready a week ago.	
17	(closing)	

Topic analysis of these two conversations reveals that Slay dominated the conversation and that Brewer's role was, at best, minimal. Both calls were initiated by Slay and all hints about the purpose of Slay's efforts were initiated by Slay. Brewer's four substantive topics were suggestions that he check around to see if he could find a pill press (twice in the first conversation), a report that he had no luck and a suggestion that Slay try to borrow one (in the second conversation). At issue, in this case, was whether or not Brewer's contributions to this conversation, minimal though they were, were enough to implicate him in the drug manufacturing process.

In the face of overwhelming evidence, some time after the tapes were made, Bob Slay pleaded guilty and agreed to work with the government in implicating others who were involved with him. Slay told the police that Brewer knew from the beginning that the chemicals he sold Slay were for the purpose of manufacturing Ecstasy.

It should be noted that Slay is never explicit in his references to the product being manufactured and he was never explicit about who his colleagues were, as table 8.1 reveals. Through statements to the police, Slay alleged that, since Brewer knew from the beginning exactly what the product was and who Slay's associates were, there was no particular need to identify them in

Table 8.1 References to product/associates in Slay–Brewer telephone conversations

Term used	Slay	Brewer
References to item produced (both calls)		
it	15	0
stuff	6	0
them	5	0
thing	1	0
son of a gun	1	0
References to Slay's associates		
Call 1		
we	9	0
they	13	0
Call 2		
we	23	0
they	5	0

these conversations. Such a position would, of course, implicate Brewer in the scheme to produce the Ecstasy.

When inexplicit information is presented in conversations such as these, it is possible that the listener never does figure out exactly what is being referred to but, for social and politeness reasons, simply goes along with the conversation anyway, even though it is not clear to the listener exactly who or what is being referred to. To Brewer's credit, he never espoused this position. His stance was that he had no knowledge of Slay's original intention to produce Ecstasy pills when the chemicals were purchased but that he inferred this from the first conversation, particularly when Slay said that he wanted to buy a pill press. Brewer's position is that his heart sank when he heard this, and that he was so uncomfortable with this new information that he could think of nothing from that point on but getting out of the conversation.

Three possible interpretations, then, could be made concerning Slay's inexplicitness:

1 *The prosecution's position*: There was no need for Slay to be
   explicit since the references to the product and Slay's associates could be inferred by Brewer from previous, untaped
   conversations when Slay and Brewer met at a barbecue.
2 *The defense position*: Brewer was able to infer Slay's intention to make Ecstasy pills after the words "pill press" were
   uttered by Slay, but there was no conversation about the
   product at the barbecue or elsewhere.
3 *Nobody's position*: Brewer never does figure out what Slay is
   getting at with his inexplicit references to the product and his
   associates.

Position 3, that Brewer simply went along with the conversation
without ever realizing what Slay meant, would have been difficult
to maintain, since Brewer responds to the "pill press" request by
offering to look for one. Although Brewer's major business was
producing chemicals for products such as ink, he was certainly
mindful of the illegality of selling chemicals to drug manufacturers.

   If the world of conversation were a simple matter of explicit
information-sharing, without the overlays of social rules, economic considerations, politeness and emotions, Brewer might have
said something like, "Oh my God, now I understand why you
bought those chemicals from me. You're making illegal drugs. I
can't get involved in anything like this. It's my duty to report this
to the police." And if he had done this, there would have been
no case against him. But even those who are officially assigned
responsibility for reporting suspected illegality, such as counsel-
ling psychologists in child abuse situations, find it risky and difficult
to do so.

   Linguists point out that certain kinds of verbal actions are
intrinsically "face-threatening," acts which by their nature are
contrary to the desires of a conversational partner. Obvious
examples include accusations, threats, ridicule, expressions of dis-
approval, insults, reprimands and challenges. Most peace-loving
people attempt to avoid face-threatening acts by engaging in
various verbal strategies of their own. Employing such "face-
saving" strategies, however, comes at some cost. For example,
by not displaying righteous indignation at someone's report of
illegal behavior, one runs the risk of appearing to condone such
behavior.

A classic example, given in chapter 1, is the ethnically inappropriate or off-color joke. Internally we may want to say, "Oh, no. Please don't tell me this offensive joke." But most people seldom manage such behavior. Even after the punch line is uttered we still have the chance to side with decency and honor by saying, "I'm sorry, but I don't laugh at ethnic or dirty jokes." Again, most of us fail this test as well. To do otherwise would be a face-threatening act. This is not to condone laughing at ethnic or dirty jokes. Rather, it attempts to explain the complexity of social interaction that inevitably accompanies such situations. Even those who politely, if uncomfortably, smile weakly at such jokes, often give hints of discomfort that can be considered as mitigated face-threatening. That is, they may quickly change the subject, turn away to talk to someone else or they may even tell what they consider to be an appropriate joke which has no ethnic or off-color components, perhaps as a model of appropriateness to the offender.

To this point, then, the issue became the extent to which Brewer shared knowledge of Slay's intentions before the conversations were tape recorded. The linguistic question concerns whether or not Brewer used conversational strategies that support his contention that he learned of Slay's real intention during the first tape recording.

Although relatively little has been written about how participants in a conversation distance themselves from what is being said, the phenomenon is an easily recognized one. Uncomfortable listeners may not be aware of exactly what strategies they are calling upon to put psychological distance between themselves and the speaker of the discomforting information but, when tape recordings of the event are available, such strategies, conscious or unconscious, can be described. If there were a video tape of a face-to-face conversation, one might observe eye-avoidance, fidgeting or actual walking away or backing off. Since the tapes in question were audio tapes of telephone conversations, however, such non-verbal evidence is not available and we must rely entirely on language evidence.

From research in other settings, we know that it is often useful to verbally distance oneself from other parties in a conversation. For example, physicians find it more comfortable, when dealing with the intimate body parts of their patients, to distance themselves by referring to a body part as "*the* vagina" rather than "*your* vagina." Another technique is to substitute "we" for "I," as in "*We* need to take a look at the incision." Such language use tends to remove the person of the physician from the already far too intimate situation.

Perhaps there is no more common example of distancing behavior than is found every day in an elevator. By unwritten but virtually universal agreement, elevator passengers face the front of the elevator and keep their eyes fixed at levels either above surrounding passengers (usually on the electronic indicator reporting the current floor level) or toward the floor. Any conversation in elevators tends to be in hushed tones and somewhat cryptic. Conversational partners are careful not to talk over or past other passengers who happen to stand between them. Since elevators, by necessity, violate what we perceive to be appropriate distances, our language and behavior work hard to preserve the appearance of normality.

Language distancing is also used in telephone conversations: one way to distance oneself is to hang up abruptly. This violates the cooperative principle in conversation, of course, and is a face-threatening act of great magnitude. Two types of distancing in conversation tend to minimize threats to face: (a) one can distance oneself from the *other speaker* by saying, for example, "That's your problem; I have nothing to do with it," (b) another type of distancing preserves the relationship with the conversational partner but attempts to distance from the *other person's topic*.

Distancing from the other speaker is far more face-threatening and far less cooperative than is distancing from the other speaker's topic. The most flagrant type of topic distancing is simply to change the subject of conversation. Since doing so runs the risk of being considered rude and actually edging over into speaker distancing (a much more face-threatening situation), most speakers use such a strategy with caution. It is far more common to retreat to silence or minimal participation.

We have already shown that Brewer brought up only 15 percent of all the substantive topics introduced in these conversations, leaving to Slay the role of topic dominator (85 percent of topics). Other measures yield similar results. Slay utters 875 words (85 percent), while Brewer produces only 159 (15 percent). Slay's utterances are considerably longer than Brewer's (14.11 words per utterance versus 2.56).

When one speaker dominates a conversation so thoroughly there are at least two possible explanations. One, as shown earlier, is that the dominating speaker is the only one with an agenda. The other explanation, not in conflict with the first, is that the non-dominant speaker is deliberately distancing him- or herself from the topic (and, therefore, from the conversation, but not from the dominant speaker) by offering minimal participation. Fifty-seven percent of Brewer's turns of talk are one-word utterances, mostly the feedback markers *uh-huh, yeah, hmm, oh, okay* and *man.*

Cooperative conversationalists hold their own in a conversation, introducing topics of their own and elaborating on these topics by providing detailed information, giving evidence and reasons for a position or opinion. It is also common in a successful conversation for one speaker even to advance the other person's topics by commenting on them and offering specifics to support or contradict them. In short, cooperative conversationalists get involved in the conversation's topics, not just their own.

Brewer's contributions to these conversations indicate little or no such involvement. He does little to advance the conversations, leaving this work entirely to Slay. For example, if Brewer were involved cooperatively, he might be expected to make reference to Slay's repeated topics. Table 8.1 shows that he did not. Although Slay is never explicit, as noted earlier, about the item to be produced or about his associates who were trying to manufacture it, Brewer never even produces an anaphoric reference. He makes no mention at all, direct or indirect, explicit or referential.

Perhaps the worst thing that can be said about Brewer's contribution to these conversations is that he offers to "check around" to see if he can help Slay locate a pill press. Eight days later, when Slay calls Brewer again, Brewer says "I haven't had any luck." On the surface it might seem that by offering to "check around," Brewer involved himself in the manufacture of an illegal product and that by later reporting that he had "no luck," Brewer had tried to find a press and not succeeded. But several aspects of these utterances are problematic. For one thing, they lack specificity and the ring of genuineness. What Brewer does *not* say is almost as interesting as what he does say. He does not give

Slay any indication that he knows how to find a pill press or where one might be located. He mentions no past experience of his own or others in such a search. He mentions no contacts and no catalogues or listings. An effective businessman does more than say "I'll try." He gives the client evidence that he knows what he's doing. Finally, eight days later, Brewer offers no elaboration on his "no luck" utterance. He does not say where he tried to look, whom he contacted, or what he heard on the street. Just as an apology containing only the words "I'm sorry" is infelicitous because it does not specify what one is sorry for and does not offer potential relief from similar offences in the future, so a minimal "I haven't had any luck" is infelicitous as a report of a failed effort. It is, once again, a minimal contribution to the conversation and one that gives us no reason to believe either that Brewer ever tried to locate a press or that he intended to look for one.

If Brewer did not intend to help Slay find a pill press, why did he appear to offer to do so? Part of distancing oneself from a topic without alienating oneself from one's conversational partner often involves hollow offers, offers that are easy enough to make, such as "I'll try," but are equally easy to conclude with acceptable failure. It is not difficult to compile a list of such hollow offers. For example, the department store is out of a specific product and offers to try to find it in one of their branch stores. You meet an acquaintance unexpectedly and as you part company, one of you says, "Let's get together for lunch." You are negotiating the price of a new car and the salesperson says, "Let me go to my boss. I'll try to get the price down a bit for you." This list can grow very long with little effort.

What distinguishes a hollow offer from a felicitous offer, in addition to the lack of specific details that legitimize it, is that the stakes for failure are not very high. One makes hollow offers only when the expectations for success are minimal and where success is not especially crucial. Brewer's "Let me check around" most certainly fits the category of a hollow offer. This is verified by Brewer's lack of the felicitous details required of a serious offer and by his lack of felicitous elaboration about what he did when he had "no luck."

In short, Brewer, like the acquaintance who tells you that some-day you'll have to get together for lunch, is not serious about his offer. His words are formulaic and, when coupled with his overall reticence to say anything at all in these conversations and his apparent unwillingness to advance the topics of Slay, give every indication of a person distancing himself from information which he didn't care to learn about but for which he was unwilling to produce a face-threatening statement of righteous indignation. Needless to say, Brewer's words do not indicate conspiracy in a plot to manufacture an illegal substance. Although his attorney was eager to present this analysis at trial, Brewer elected to plead guilty to minor charges rather than face the trauma of the courtroom.

9

Asking Questions

One of the most common things that occur in conversation is question asking. We ask many types of questions: requests for information, requests for opinions, requests for procedures and requests for clarification, among others. Sometimes, especially with teachers, the question is not really a search for factual information. Rather, the question is a kind of test to see whether or not the person will answer what we want them to answer. Other times, as with media interviews, the questioner is genuinely trying to discover new information.

On the surface, it might seem that questions and answers are totally separate things. But this is seldom the case. The *way* a question is asked can influence or even determine the answer given. In much of life this does not make a great deal of difference but, in matters of law, the possible influence of a question on the answer can have tremendously important consequences. Lawyers have long recognized the dangers of "leading questions," for example, and the courts try to prevent this from happening. If a witness is asked a leading question, the opposition attorney has the right to object and cause the question to be deleted or changed. This type of question has been discussed earlier, particularly in the case of Steven Suyat's perjury charge as well as in the case of Larry Gentry. But attorneys are not the only ones to be tempted to use leading questions.

Police interrogations follow the same question–answer framework. A suspected criminal, when apprehended, is interviewed by one or more policemen and asked to recall exactly what happened. In such circumstances there is usually no attorney present to make sure that the questions are not loaded. As we have seen in Larry Gentry's case (chapter 6), his simple volunteering to help the police turned into a nightmare which led to his indictment for assisting in a murder. In Steven Suyat's case (chapter 7), the fact that he was subpoenaed as a witness for the prosecution essentially guaranteed that no attorney would be representing his own best interests in that trial. Both Gentry and Suyat were damaged severely by the way questions were put to them in events for which they were, as laymen to the law, and as inarticulate users of the language, very vulnerable.

Those who are weak, including the uneducated, the very young and the mentally handicapped, are particularly susceptible to being led by the questions of attorneys or police. This chapter outlines some of the question–answer problems encountered by Jerry Townsend, a 29-year-old black retarded adult who was accused of multiple rape–murder charges in Florida, as well as the problems encountered by children when they are interviewed in criminal cases.

Was Jerry Townsend really answering questions?

Jerry Townsend clearly admitted on tape to killing as many as five prostitutes in the general areas of Fort Lauderdale and Miami. Since there was, in 1978, a multitude of unsolved murders of women in these metropolitan areas, the police probed Townsend for his possible involvement in these other cases as well.

Before discussing their questioning of Townsend, the report of a Miami psychologist is instructive. Dr Frank Loeffler of Miami spent almost five hours with Townsend after his apprehension, administering intelligence tests, Rorschalk tests, the Bender Gestalt tests and other diagnostic instruments. His report notes that Townsend showed a "low level of mental functioning and/or brain damage." The doctor believed that the right side of Townsend's brain was damaged since he drew inverse pictures in response to the drawing tests. Townsend's drawing of a human figure was diagnosed at the level of a 3 to 4-year-old. On reading tests, Townsend scored at the second grade level, "within the range of mild mental retardation." His arithmetic scores were at the first grade level. On the Wechsler intelligence test, Townsend scored a 57 (a score of 55 is considered mentally retarded). The Rorschalk test also diagnosed him as mentally retarded. Dr Loeffler's report also noted that Townsend was not malingering or faking. He genuinely tried to make a good impression. The psychologist's conclusion was that Townsend functioned at the level of a 7 or 8-year-old child.

Townsend had little or no concept of time and had neither the emotional nor cognitive ability to understand what was happening to him. Townsend gave conflicting information about many things, including his age when he got married (age 25, then age 17), how old his daughter was (8, then 5), the year of his marriage separation (1977, then 1972) and the age at which he finished high school (22, then 25; even though, in fact, he only went to ninth grade).

Dr Richard Cabrera, a clinical psychologist, also evaluated Townsend and stated that the suspect was not competent to understand the rational and factual proceedings against him: "His intellectual capacities are so limited that one cannot, with any confidence, accept any actual statement that he may have made, particularly if it has any reference to time or place or names or any details of even an elementary nature." Dr Cabrera's analysis concluded that Townsend had an IQ of 58 (mental retardation), and that he functioned at the age of a 6 to 7-year-old child. The findings of Dr Loeffler and Dr Cabrera were collaborated by a psychiatrist, Dr Mario Martinez, who also diagnosed Townsend as mentally retarded and agreed essentially with the two psychologists.

The prosecution offered their experts to counter Drs Loeffler, Cabrera and Martinez. Psychologist Leslie Alker's diagnosis was essentially the same regarding Townsend's IQ ("51 or so"), but he claimed that Townsend functioned at the level of a 19-year-old. Discovering that Mr Alker was not licensed and did not hold a doctorate, the judge then ruled Alker not an expert. This did not stop him from offering his opinions, however.

Perhaps only outsiders to the unusual ways in which courtrooms operate will find it odd that, having been declared not an expert, Alker was able to continue to present his conclusions anyway. The only difference in the court procedure, oddly enough, was that the defense attorney was prevented from cross-examining him on the grounds that Alker was not an expert. Such reasoning defies the logic of the layman but appears to be common in the courtroom communication system.

Additional expert psychiatrists, Dr Sanford Jacobson and Dr William Corwin, essentially supported Mr Alker's opinions. Dr Jacobson observed that he did not perform psychological testing and that he found the grade equivalency that someone operates at a "foolish, absurd concept." He agreed, however, that there was much to doubt about Townsend's ability to place things in sequence and his concept of time. He also concluded that Townsend had "the sufficient present ability to consult with his attorneys with a reasonable degree of rational understanding." Dr Corwin substantiated this, noting that Townsend responded to him during his one-hour interview "in a rational and coherent manner. He understood my questions and gave coherent responses to them." Dr Corwin agreed with Dr Jacobson that Townsend had a rational and factual understanding of the proceedings in which he was currently involved.

This psychological profile of Jerry Townsend is important as we examine the interrogation of Townsend by the Dade County police. Although there was disagreement between the defense and prosecution experts concerning the age level at which Townsend could function, there was no disagreement about his intelligence. He was apparently retarded.

There was apparently no disagreement between the defense and the prosecution about Townsend's guilt in committing at least one, and probably more, rape–murders of area prostitutes. Further probing determined that Townsend was very much afraid that his daughter might grow up to be a prostitute also. His murder (or murders) was apparently part of a personal crusade to rid the world of prostitutes so that there would be no such occupation for his daughter to follow. Clearly such a person should be institutionalized. The essential question was – should it be a prison or a mental institution?

Jerry Townsend never came to trial in Dade County since he was first tried for similar crimes in Fort Lauderdale. Whatever his guilt may have been, the evidence against him remains a monument of unfair question-asking techniques, as the following will indicate.

The Dade County police interrogated Townsend over a period of five days, from September 6 to September 10, 1979. Only parts of each day's interrogation were tape recorded, leaving the nagging question about what was said that was *not* recorded on any given day. On 24 occasions during the four tapings, the tape recorder was turned off. On ten of these instances, the police note that they are turning it off but on 14 occasions, no note is made whatsoever. The result of such on-off signatures is to impeach the tape. For example, on September 6 we hear Townsend saying the following:

> Uh-uh. That's (*tape off, tape on*). Walk down about one block, come up through there.

The government's transcript of Towsend's utterance (or utterances) gives the impression that this was a continuous sentence. The transcript read as follows:

> Uh-uh. That's walk down about one block, come up through there.

Although there are electronic methods of determining whether a break in the tape occurred between his words, *that's* and *walk*, other more obvious clues make this unnecessary. The audible click of the tape recorder's on-off switch is one. Background noise change is another. A dog had been barking for a minute or so up to the word *that's*. By the time Townsend uttered *walk*, the dog suddenly had stopped. In addition, there is a noticeable difference in volume between his softly spoken "Uh-uh. That's" and the much louder remainder of the utterance. Sudden topic shifts are another indication of on-off signatures, accompanied, of course, by other clues. At one point on the September 10 recording, for example, the detective and Townsend are arguing over whether or not the detective had manipulated Townsend into talking with the Fort Lauderdale police. At this point, the tape recorder is shut off in the middle of one of Townsend's sentences. When the tape comes back on, they are talking about three girls in Tampa. Occasionally, after a tape break, the voice returns with an answer to a question which is not on the tape. After an announced break for coffee, for example, the taping begins with Townsend saying, "I mean 77." At issue here, linguistically, is for what question is Townsend's answer? When the tape is turned off and on, we cannot be certain that his answer is actually to the preceding question.

Evidence of Townsend's mental weaknesses can be seen regularly even in the words he uses to describe events or things. His idiosyncratic way of describing "killing," for example, is "commit suicide." In one rather telling part of the September 6 tape recording, after informing the detectives that he had killed a woman with a little piece of wire, one of the detectives asked him what he did with her clothes. Townsend responds:

Townsend: Well, those short pants. I took the pants and her blouse and just got rid of the whole thing.
Detective: Jerry, I think you're getting a little confused.
(*Tape turned off. Tape turned on.*)
Townsend: And the time I got through with five minutes of her time, that's when I commit suicide. — Killed her

It should be pointed out that Townsend's "five minutes of her time" is used consistently to mean "had sexual intercourse." At this point, the detective asks Townsend again what he choked the woman with.

Townsend: With her bra.
Detective: Okay. And you still left the sock in her mouth, is that right?

To this point, there had been no mention of a sock being in the woman's mouth. The fact that the detective used the definite article, *the*, before *sock* rather than the indefinite article, *a*, indicates this clearly. In English, one uses definite articles (i.e. "the sock") to refer to objects or people previously referred to. Since the detective used the definite article, it is clear that he and Townsend had been discussing the sock during the time when the tape recorder was shut off.

If this use of the definite article were not enough, the detective also uses the word, *still*, presupposing that something had already taken place or something had already been said. The most likely time that Townsend may have straightened out his story was when the tape was off, after the detective had told him that he was "getting a little confused."

It seems inconceivable that the police should be allowed to turn a tape recorder off whenever they are not getting what they want out of a suspect. When the tape was turned off, Townsend might have started to forget the lines that possibly had been prepared for him by the police about a crime that he did not commit. Even if this is *not* the case, the police have opened themselves up to the suspicion that this was what they were doing.

It would be even more damaging to the prosecution if Townsend had actually said something on tape which the detectives found damaging to their case and so they stopped the tape, rewound it to where they wanted it, then taped over the unfavorable parts with newly prompted information. Again, we do not know that this was the case, but their constant on-off signatures lead to such suspicions.

A similar situation occurred in the September 10 taping. As noted earlier, Townsend had complained that the detective had turned him over to the Fort Lauderdale police without his permission. To this, the detective responds:

> *Detective*: But it's up to you whether you go with anyone or
>   not.
> *Townsend*: No, I –
>   (*Tape turned off. Tape turned on.*)
> *Detective*: Right here, tell me straight out the truth about these
>   three girls that were shot in Tampa.

Townsend's effort to continue his protest will never be known because his words were cut off (and possibly even recorded over) by the person hitting the off button. If Townsend had completed a denial that he went willingly, the government's case would have been severely weakened. By cutting Townsend off, the police were either guilty of tampering with the tape or giving the appearance of having done so.

Once again, we have Townsend's answer to a question, "And the time I got through with five minutes of her time, that's when I commit suicide." The problem, caused by the tape being turned off and on, is that we do not know the question that Townsend's answer responded to. We do not and cannot know how long the tape recorder was off. Only from the conversation that follows can we get clear pieces of information about what was discussed off the record.

At issue in the pre-trial hearings for this case was whether or not Jerry Townsend was mentally competent to help his own lawyers with his defense and whether or not he had a rational and factual understanding of the proceedings with which he was then involved. The testimony of the psychiatrists and psychologists, noted earlier, spoke to these issues. From his four taped conversations with the police, it is clear that Townsend answered not one question having to do with the specifics of time, place, or names of persons. When he does specify such things, it is not in response to specific questions but, rather, as a self-generated afterthought. Even then, there is no consistency in the things about which Townsend is specific. For example, on the second day of taping, the detectives ask the name of the girl that Townsend is describing. He says that he does not know. Later, he refers to her as Darlene. Still later, she is someone else. On the first day of taping, Townsend first explains that he choked all five girls at a baseball park. Three minutes later, however, he says that he did *not* take them to the ballpark and that all of them were killed in different ways.

There are three major potential reasons for the inconsistency of Townsend's statement on these tapes:

1 The question-asking technique influenced Townsend's answers.
2 Townsend did not have the mental ability to keep the facts straight.
3 Townsend was lying.

If the tape recorder had not been switched off and on so many times we may have found more inconsistency in his answers. There are times in which Townsend describes a victim as a black girl with a white Stingray. Off goes the tape and the next words we hear are Townsend saying that it was a white girl in a black Stingray.

Although it may be the case that most suspects in Townsend's position might be expected to be liars, there is little reason to believe this here. For one thing, Townsend would be the worst liar imaginable. A good liar must, above all else, keep his story straight. Secondly, he must lie to prevent the worst from happening. Townsend has already admitted to murder. The point of lying from this juncture would be, to the most accomplished liar, futile. This leaves two possibilities to explain the inconsistencies of his answers: his lack of mental ability (which was asserted by the defense expert psychiatrists) or the way the questions were put to him by the police.

Linguistic analysis does not enable one to make technical conclusions about mental abilities. It can point out inconsistencies in the language used but conclusions about mental ability are generally left to experts in other fields. Linguistics *does* deal with question–answer strategies, however, particularly the ways in which questions have influence on responses.

Serious issues in the Townsend case were the following:

1 Were Jerry Townsend's words on tape actually answers to questions? Or was the tape spliced together to make it appear that way?
2 Were Jerry Townsend's alleged answers actually his *own* answers? Or were they prompting's and suggestions by the police?
3 Were Jerry Townsend's inconsistent responses a result of his own limited mental capacity? Or were his changed answers influenced by his questioners?

Inaccurately restating the subject's words

It is common in interviews for the questioner to restate the response of the interviewee. There is nothing essentially wrong with such a procedure, as long as the restatements are accurate. The detectives interviewing Jerry Townsend, however, were often inaccurate in their efforts to restate Townsend's words. For example, consider the following:

Detective: Jerry, did you kill these girls up there in Fort Lauderdale?
Townsend: No, I didn't commit suicide but, you know, I just put them where they can't be of a use no more.
Detective: In other words, you just went ahead and choked them around the neck? Now you have to be straight out.
Townsend: Yeah. Yeah.

In terms of interviewing technique, the detective leaves a great deal to be desired. It might appear that he has got Townsend to agree that he choked the girls in Fort Lauderdale. But, for one thing, the detective's restatement is nowhere near what Townsend actually said. It is, at best, an interpretation. The detective's technique then, is to follow his restatement with an urge to be honest. To this, Townsend says "yeah, yeah." The *recency principle* (noted in chapter 6) argues that when two or more questions are asked, the response is to the last, or most recent, one. Is Townsend agreeing that what he meant by "put them where they can't be of a use no more" was actually, as the detective puts it, that he choked them to death? Not likely (although it *is* likely that Townsend actually killed someone). The detective contaminated any useful understanding we might have of Townsend's words by: (a) inaccurately restating and (b) using a multiple question sequence which casts doubt on Townsend's agreement to the crime. The inaccurate, interpretive restatement was a poor question-asking strategy; the multiple question sequence only compounded the matter. These interviews contained a multitude of both.

Playing on cooperative behavior

The Townsend interviews are remarkable for many things, not least of which is the suspect's utter cooperativeness. Not many suspects are so willing to admit to everything suggested to them by the police. We have already noted how Townsend changes his answers after the tape recorder has been switched off and on. But even during a series of questions uninterrupted by the on–off switch, Townsend's cooperative behavior is unusual. For example:

Detective: Okay. What about the others? Where did they take place?
Townsend: Same place where this here one took place here.
Detective: Something like a railroad track?
Townsend: Yeah.
Detective: Or an old house or something?
Townsend: Yeah.

At the time of this interview, the detectives are sitting with Townsend in the Miami police station. They had just finished discussing a murder he committed at a baseball park. At issue is

what Townsend might mean by "This here one took place here."
It is not likely that he meant that he killed other girls at the
Miami police station, even though this might be argued from
Townsend's use of "here." A better argument might be that
Townsend was referring to the baseball park, since it is the im-
mediately preceding locale. In any case, Townsend certainly did
not refer to a railroad track or an old house.

To a later listener, the detective's question sequence seems
bizarre. It is unclear why he redirected the locale reference from
the ballpark, then to a railroad track, then to an old house. What
is even more bizarre, however, is that Townsend agrees to all
these locales. It seems bizarre, that is, until we notice Townsend's
extremely cooperative behavior throughout the interviews.

He cooperates *so* much, in fact, that this too becomes bizarre.
Overcooperative behavior can be as aberrant as uncooperative
behavior. Townsend appears to be willing to agree to anything
at all. To him, cooperation is more important than truth. The
result is a bonanza for any investigator who may wish to clear
his slate of unresolved crime. The down side is that Townsend's
testimony becomes unbelievable. Thus, what might seem, on the
surface at least, to be clear incriminating evidence actually becomes
doubtful since Jerry Townsend would apparently agree to having
committed most of the unsolved murders in Dade County.

The question–answer sequence is one of the most powerful
tools of human communication. We tend to accept questions and
answers at face value, however, and often we do not examine
them carefully. A law case, such as Jerry Townsend's, causes us
to look more closely at this tool. Thanks to tape recorders, what
may appear to be a question–answer sequence may simply be
reconstructed or put together out of sequence, after the fact.
Likewise, what may *appear* to be an answer may be, in the case
of an overcooperative and unintelligent subject, little more than
a prompted or suggested response. And, finally, the way a set of
questions is posed can make it appear that agreement to the substantive question has been achieved when, in fact, such agreement is only to a minor point which just happened to be asked
last in a sequence.

Was Jerry Townsend really answering questions? There is no
way to ever really know. Even his public defenders suspected that
Townsend had committed murder. But how many, or when, we

will probably never know. His pathological cooperativeness is one hindrance to the answer. The bungled interviewing by the police is another barrier. Before his trial in Miami came up, Jerry Townsend was tried for multiple murders in Fort Lauderdale. He is currently serving a life sentence in prison – probably not the right type of institution for such a person.

Questioning a 3-year-old

Child sexual abuse cases pose a challenge to the skills of law enforcement officers in asking children questions. Children tend to be fearful, even traumatized by adult interviews. Their memories are not always consistent and their testimony is frequently considered unreliable. But there are essentially only two types of evidence in most child sexual abuse cases: medical evidence and witness testimony. Expert child molesters take advantage of this fact and see to it that no adults witness the abuse. Medical testimony is often disputed with physicians for each side giving contradictory opinions. In such cases, a great burden falls on the shoulders of the person who conducts the fact-finding interview with the only witness available, the child who was abused.

Police departments conventionally interview both the accused and the victims in cases involving criminal charges. Theoretically at least, the ability of police investigators is adequate enough to provide verbal evidence for the arrest of a suspect. That ability, however, exists only for *adult* suspects and witnesses. Traditionally, the police are not skilled at interviewing children. Recognizing this problem, law enforcement agencies have gone to social workers and child psychologists for help in this matter. On the surface, this appears to be a sensible thing to do. With the multitude of recent child sexual abuse cases, however, it has become clear that the current practice of child interviewer teams (called Child Protection Teams) is still not adequate.

Specialists within this field recognize their deficiencies and are busily conducting studies to improve the practice. Dr Sue White, for example, of the Case Western Reserve University Hospital, is among the researchers trying to find answers to the difficult questions about how to interview small children in such cases.

As usual, one good place to begin such a study is with previous tape-recorded interviews. It is useful to first discover what has been done badly or ineffectively, then to try to improve the procedure. A second idea is to obtain the perspective and knowledge of other areas of expertise. Few if any linguists, for example, have been working on the special problems of interviewing small children in sexual abuse cases. In late 1985, I was asked by an attorney to assist him in the defense of a client who was charged with sexually abusing his 3-year-old daughter (all references to names and places will be changed here to preserve the anonymity of the victims).

I had listened to thousands of tape-recorded conversations and interviews in my academic career, but as I listened to this one, it seemed that it was one of the most inept interviewing styles I had ever heard. Or was it? I was considering this interview a police interrogation, a fact-finding probe of a witness. As such, it was a failure. But if I had considered it as social work, a therapeutic interview, I might have thought better of it. And it was exactly this point that caused this interview to fail: it was neither a therapeutic nor a fact-probing interview.

In the child sexual abuse case I worked on, the State child protection team interviewer interspersed the following types of comments throughout her interview with 3-year-old Diana:

• Well we're going to protect you.
• We're not going to let him do that to you anymore.
• Because we don't want him to do that to you do we?

Not only did the interviewer err in mixing the therapeutic interview with the interrogation interview, but her switching occurred when she misheard or misunderstood the child's complaint that she, the interviewer, would not let the child play with the other toys any longer:

Interviewer	*Child*
Let's put them right there, okay?	
We'll put them right there and let them watch us. Wanna	

hold my hand while we finish
talking?

You're gonna take all the toys
huh? That's Winnie the Pooh.

Listen. We're gonna put this
right over here.

And we'll play with that when
we're through with the dollies,
okay?

We need to finish playing with
the dollies. Did your daddy
ever put his pee-pee in your
mouth?

He did?

You don't want him to do that
anymore?

Well, we're going to protect
you. We're not going to let
him do that to you anymore.
Because we don't want him to
do that to you, do we?

Put this in there.

This go here.

Aw.

No.

Nah.

Yeah. They don't let me
play with it anymore.

No.

Nope.

Not only does the interviewer misunderstand the child, but
also the child misunderstands the interviewer. The toys had been
removed, much to the girl's dismay. Abruptly, the interviewer
asks the direct question about her father's pee-pee. The girl's
apparent inconsistent responses ("Nah" followed by "Yeah") are
actually consistent with her focus on the toy prohibition. When
the girl complains that they don't let her play with them anymore,
the interviewer, remembering her preceding question about her
daddy's pee-pee, hears this as meaning that the child does not

want her father to do that anymore. Sensing trauma, the interviewer follows good social work practice, but weak interrogation practice, and shifts into a therapeutic interview.

A therapeutic interview is, by definition, a helping interview. It is one in which the interviewer takes the side of the other person. It is filled with sympathy and compassion. While this may be a good thing, it proves difficult for evaluating the information being obtained. With its justifiable client-centered bias, the therapeutic interview is an inappropriate information-gathering procedure. This bias of the interviewer above is highlighted by her mishearing or misunderstanding. She perceived trauma when disappointment about the toy removal was all that was indicated. In the courtroom, this interviewer was severely criticized for doing the thing she had been well trained to do, but which, for the purposes of a trial, was totally inappropriate.

The suggestion of experts in the field of child sexual abuse interviewing is to keep the interrogation/information interview separate from the therapeutic interview. Do the interrogation first; then do the therapy. One simply has to discover the truth about what happened before therapy can begin. Many interviewers jump the gun in this and, in doing so, both reveal their own legal bias and become poor witnesses for the prosecution.

In all conversation, the participants have points of view, perspectives, understandings of the past and present which guide or influence their perceptions about what the other person says or means to say. For example, if a married woman who had been seeing a boyfriend were to say to her close female friend, "*He* came to my house today," the friend might well understand "he" to refer to the boyfriend. There is nothing in the words or grammar of English to give this clue. Only the context of their lives could make this clear. If that same married woman had a malfunctioning refrigerator and told her husband, after he got home from the office, "He came today," the unsuspecting husband might understand "he" to mean the repairman. Again, there is nothing in the words or grammar of English to give this clue. Only the context of their lives makes it clear and comprehensible. This sort of contextual understanding is referred to by linguists and cognitive psychologists as "schema." Others, notably sociologists and anthropologists call the same thing "frames," as in frames of reference.

Thus, a person who asks a question does so from a schema or frame of reference. On the other hand, the person who answers a question also has his or her schema, or frame of reference, which may or may not match that of the questioner. In the case of Larry Gentry (chapter 6), we saw the different schemas of Gentry and the prosecutors. It was clear that these two men were operating from quite different perspectives, causing considerable miscommunication. When an adult asks questions of a child, the opportunities for miscommunication increase greatly, largely because it is extremely difficult to know what a child is thinking. The interviewer needs to put her/himself in the shoes of the child, to try to see the world from that child's context and perspective and to realize that the child's ability to verbalize his or her feelings and knowledge is limited by a number of factors.

In order to get the child to tell what has actually happened in the experience suspected to have been child sexual abuse, child protection team interviewers frequently begin with a period of playing with the child, often using what are called anatomically correct dolls. These dolls attempt to replicate the physical features, particularly the sexual organs, of adult as well as child males and females. The dolls have clothing which can be removed as part of the play event. Part of the reason for such play is to get the child to use her own words for the body parts, such as the penis, breasts, buttocks and vagina. In that way, the interviewer can adopt the child's terminology to make sure that they are both referring to the same things. A second purpose of the doll play is to get the child to self-generate or act out alleged sexual abuse by means of the dolls. In this way, the interviewer can see what the child does with the dolls, particularly with their sexual parts and then ask the child questions based on this acted out demonstration.

The most difficult aspect of the child sexual abuse interview, especially for children under five or six years old, is to shift the child's play schema, once it has been established as doll play, to a past event schema, one in which the alleged sexual abuse took place. The differentiation or connection between the schemas of the present and the past is much clearer to adults, possibly because we have so much past to compare with the present. To make things more difficult, small children naturally prefer the schema of play to almost any adult schema. The interview procedure was set up to ease the transfer from present play to the past, real event. It is based on the theoretically sound assumption that we should start with children *where they are*. Unfortunately, however, children like the schema where they are (in play) so much that they want to stay there, and they resist adult efforts to move them from the concrete here and now to the abstract past.

In the child sexual abuse interview analyzed here, this effort to move the child's schema from the play event to the past actual event displays just how difficult this task can be. At this point in the interview, almost eight minutes have elapsed since the tape recorder was turned on.

		Current play event	Past real event
Intvr:	Yep. That one looks like a daddy, doesn't it?	X	
Child:	Daddy pee-pee right there.	X	
Intvr:	Is that his pee-pee?	X	
Child:	Yes.	X	
Intvr:	I see. Have you ever seen your daddy's pee-pee?		X
Child:	Yes.	?	?
Intvr:	Did your daddy touch you somewhere?		X
Child:	Yep.	?	?
Intvr:	Can you point to where he touched you?		X
Child:	Yep. Got the boobies right there.	X	
Intvr:	Yeah. Which doll do you think this one is? That's a mommy, isn't it?	X	
Child:	Yes. There's a big pee-pee.	X	
Intvr:	Can this be your daddy?	X	
Child:	Yeah.	X	
Intvr:	And this be you?	X	
	And can you show me what your daddy did?		X
Child:	That's my mommy right there.	X	
Intvr:	Okay. Now that can be mommy.	X	
	Now, if this doll's you and this one is your daddy, can you show me what he did?		X
Child:	Yeah. This, this goes right here-	X	

Intvr:	Look, if this is you. Let's put this right		
	over here 'til we're finished, okay?	X	
	If this is you and this is your daddy doll	X	
Child:	That's not a girl.	X	
Intvr:	Uh-huh. Right. And that's the mommy,		
	can you show me –		X
Child:	(*unintelligible*)	?	?
Intvr:	Did you say your daddy touched your		
	butt?		X
Child:	Yeah.	?	?
Intvr:	And then, if this is the daddy doll and		
	this is you, can you show me what he		
	did to you?		X
Child:	I, me, me, uh, mommy and daddy.	X	
Intvr:	This is a daddy doll?	X	

In the above passage in the interview, every effort by the interviewer to transfer from the current play event schema to the real, past event schema is successfully thwarted by the child, who is clearly more interested in playing than in talking about alleged past sexual abuse. The responses categorized with question marks are ones in which it is not clear whether the child was referring to the play event or the past event. Since the interviewer has not made it clear whether seeing daddy's pee-pee refers to the daddy doll or the child's real daddy, the child's answer of "yes" is ambiguous. The same is true of the child's answer to the interviewer's vague question, "Did your daddy touch you somewhere?" We get a strong hint of the child's reference, however, in her answer to the interviewer's follow-up question, "Can you point to where he touched you?" To this the child is clearly pointing to the mommy doll, since her answer refers to "the boobies." This child clearly does not have the same schema as the interviewer, even with respect to the gender of the dolls, much less on the topic of where her daddy may have touched her. Strong evidence that the child maintains a schema of play is found in the interviewer's following three questions, in which the interviewer herself returns to the play schema and attempts once again to make the transfer to the past event schema: "And can you show me what your daddy did?" The child will have no part of this and identifies the mommy doll in her response.

Once again the interviewer tries to make the schema transfer:

"Can you show me what he did?" The child's answer, "This goes right here," might be considered an effort to juxtapose the sex organs of two dolls except for the fact that the interviewer's next question clearly indicates her frustration with the child's words. She begins with "Look," a word which, in this context, indicates that the interviewer considers the child's response as off-topic. This is followed by a directive to "put this right over here 'til we're finished," a sentence which now clearly identifies the child's "This goes right here" as a reference to some irrelevant toys or other dolls which diverted the child from the interviewer's goal.

The interviewer then regroups with her identification of the dolls and asks the child to show her once again what happened. The child's unintelligible response yields a request for clarification by the interviewer: "Did you say your daddy touched your butt?" This question is very curious for although the child's exact words were inaudible, they contained no more than two syllables. There is no way that two syllables, no matter what they were, could produce something like "Daddy touched my butt." The child's unintelligible utterance, in fact, contained none of the recognizable vowels found in the words "daddy," "touched," or "butt." It is sometimes difficult to imagine how people hear what they hear, but there is nothing in the interviewer's request for clarification that can be justified by the unintelligible sounds made by the child.

It appears, in fact, that the interviewer's schema is one of daddy's guilt, regardless of what the child actually says. One can only assume that the interviewer's question was not based on the child's response but, instead, on some previous statement or partial statement which, at this point, the interviewer is recycling. In any case, the child's answer, "yeah," is ambiguous since her preceding six responses as well as her following ones were in the play schema, introducing the strong likelihood that her "yeah" here referred to the *dolls* touching each other on the butt. There are other reasons to discount the possibility that the child was indicating a schema of sexual abuse, as will be discussed later.

The point of this sample passage, however, is to demonstrate how difficult it is to make the cognitive, schema transfer from the here and now to the past event. Such transfer becomes somewhat easier with children of school age, but with pre-school children it may not be possible at all. Child protection teams, in fact, make no claim that anatomically correct dolls can produce a schema transfer with pre-school children. For this age group, these dolls are primarily useful only for determining the child's labels for human body parts.

Those who carry out child sexual abuse interviews are advised to try to use language that a child can understand. This means avoiding adult words, especially Latinate ones, long sentence constructions, the passive voice, participial verbs and other complex language. Great care is taken to determine, through the use of the anatomically correct dolls, the actual words used by the child and then to use the child's terms to refer to body parts.

One subtle but very important grammatical construction, however, is not discussed in the child interviewing literature: prepositions. One of the most difficult categories of English for non-English speakers to learn is English prepositions. They are deceptive since native speakers use prepositions effectively without really thinking about it, assuming that others will understand them, especially since prepositions are so short and easy to pronounce.

The acquisition of prepositions by children, however, is much more complex than we imagine. There are, essentially, four types of prepositions, categorized by semantic content:

1 *Locative prepositions.* As the title indicates, such prepositions show location in two- or three-dimensional space. When we say "the doll is *on* the grass" we are indicating where it is located or placed, a two-dimensional relationship. But when we say "the doll is *in* the grass," we are indicating three dimensions: the doll on the grass, but also surrounded by the grass. Three-dimensional preposition meaning is obviously more complex than two-dimensional meaning.

2 *Connective prepositions.* Such prepositions show the relationship of two or more things to each other, or connection. Examples include: "Put it *with* the dollies," and "I had on pajamas."

3 *Attributive prepositions.* These prepositions carry the meaning of attribution, one dimension being the attribute of another (rather than being located with it or connected to it). Examples are the sentences: "What's this a picture *of*?" and "She is ready *for* her bath."

Table 9.1   Distribution of preposition type used by interviewer and child

Preposition	Interviewer		Child	
	No.	%	No.	%
Locative	46	60	14	70
Connective	11	14	6	30
Attributive	9	12	0	
Agentive	11	14	0	
Total	77		20	

4 *Agentive prepositions.* Such prepositions carry the meaning of an agent of the action, as opposed to an attribute, location or connection. One person or thing is the agent for doing something to someone or something else. Examples are: "He did that *to* you," "touched *with* his finger" and "Show me *with* the dolls."

Children acquire or learn English prepositions in the order given above. First they learn the locative meanings, then the connectives, next the attributives and, finally, the agentives.

In the interview with Diana, the interviewer used a total of 77 prepositions and the child used 20. This difference in number is not surprising since the adult talks more than the child. What is significant about their difference in prepositions, however, is their distribution according to these four types (table 9.1).

Even if we know nothing about how children acquire preposition semantics, table 9.1 of actual prepositions used would be revealing. It is clear that in a child sexual abuse case, it is extremely important to learn who did it and how it was done. That is, we need to learn about attribution and agent. If the child has not yet acquired the attributive and agentive meanings of prepositions, there is little likelihood of obtaining a meaningful response by using such preposition types in the questions asked. A child who does not herself use attributes and agentives is not likely to understand them.

But, since receptive competence (the ability to understand)

precedes productive competence (the ability to use) in most language learning, it is necessary to test further our assumption that this pre-school child did not comprehend the interviewer's attributive and agentive prepositions. This further test was done by analyzing responses to each question containing an agentive or attributive preposition. Criteria for assuming the child's comprehension were relevance of response, consistency of answers to the same question and whether or not the child responded at all. In this particular interview, the child answered all questions containing attributive or agentive prepositions inadequately, using these three criteria. Thus, not only did the child have no productive competence of such prepositions, but she also had no receptive competence of them. She simply did not understand the questions.

There were many other problems in the interview with Diana beside those noted here. Most flagrant, perhaps, was when the interviewer inaccurately restated what the child had just said. It is common in talking with children to repeat what they say as a kind of check on the accuracy of one's hearing or perception. As a child gets older and more experienced with language interaction, the child begins to understand that when an adult restates, it is the child's task to say whether or not the restatement is accurate. It is not known at exactly what age this type of evaluation of the adult restatement becomes understood, but it is clear that 3-year-old Diana had not yet acquired it. The following section of the interview illustrates not only the questioner's inaccurate restatements but also her schema of the guilt of Diana's father.

In this interview analyzed, the child attempts to describe an event in which her daddy spanked her. About half-way through a 21-minute interview, she introduces a spanking which was on "both sides of her butt." It is possible that the child is referring to a spanking given by the daddy doll to the child doll but, in this case, there is other evidence to indicate that it relates to a real happening. Shortly before spanking is mentioned explicitly, however, there is a confusing passage in which the child gives contradictory information. The subsequent text is as follows:

Interviewer	*Child*
Did your daddy ever touch you there in your butt?	No.
Did he ever touch you there?	Yep.

Did he touch you with his pee-pee?	Yeah.
Did he put his pee-pee inside your butt?	Yep.
Where were you when that happened?	What?
Where were you when he did that?	Daddy sets.
And daddy did it?	Yeah.
Did it hurt you?	Uh-huh.
Did daddy hurt you?	No.
Where were you in your house when he did that?	Uh, daddy spanked, daddy.
Daddy did what?	He spanked his back.
He spanked his butt?	Yeah.
How did he do that?	They make it work.
Make it worse?	Yeah.
Oh. So did you tell me that your daddy put this-	Both sides of my butt, right there.
He put it inside your butt?	Yeah.
One time or more than one?	One time.
Did you cry?	Yes.
Do you remember where you were?	I put on jommies.
Where was your mommy?	In the couch.
Was it night time or day time?	Night time.
Was your mommy in the same room or a different room?	Same room.
Was mommy sleeping or awake?	Sleeping.
Did he do it one time or lots of times?	Uh, one time.

However tempting it might seem to discount the child's testimony because of her conflicting answers to two sets of questions in this sequence, it is clear that something happened that was memorable enough for the child to generate information about. The interviewer was reasonably successful in some things, such as providing alternatives for the child to select ("one time or more than one," "night time or day time," "sleeping or awake," and "same room or different room"). On the other hand, it is also clear that the interviewer did not get the drift of the child's contextual meaning. Instead of taking the child's report of a spanking, however inarticulately she expressed it, at face value, the interviewer constructed a schema of sexual abuse. When a person has such a frame of reference, it can cause that person to hear things as supporting that frame, and to overlook the meaning conveyed by the larger context.

There are many ways to detect misperception caused by such a frame of mind, including the restatements of the child's words by the interviewer. Although it is generally regarded as acceptable practice to restate the child's words in the form of a confirmation question, one basic rule is that such restatements be accurate. In the above passage, the interviewer restates inaccurately four times, as follows:

Child: Daddy sets.
Intvr: And daddy did it?
Child: He spanked his back.
Intvr: He spanked his butt?
Child: They make it work.
Intvr: Make it worse?
Child: Both sides of my butt, right there.
Intvr: He put it inside of your butt?

By changing "daddy sets" to "daddy did it," "his back" to "his butt," "work" to "worse" and "both sides" to "inside," the interviewer evidences clear bias toward the guilt of the father which was not indicated in the child's actual words. Their frames of reference were different and their understandings of each other are confused.

Had the interviewer not been so predisposed to her schema of the father's guilt, she might have recalled an earlier discussion in the tape when the child described playing with a doctor set with her daddy. Thus, the child's reference to "daddy sets" (imperfect as it is) might not have been misperceived as "daddy did it." Likewise, had the interviewer attended to the developing context she might not have changed the child's "back" to "butt," "work" to "worse" and "both sides of my butt" to "inside of your butt."

It is also clear that the interviewer was unaware of the established knowledge in the field of child sexual abuse that the verb "touch," to a pre-school child, is always connected to hands or fingers. Thus, expressions such as "touch you with his pee-pee" are somewhat meaningless to a 3-year-old and any response given, positive or negative, is not to be trusted as valid or true.

Since touching relates directly to hands in the small child's frame of reference, the interviewer's question "Did he ever touch you in your butt?" must be understood to mean, "Did your daddy use *his hand* to touch your butt?" This, of course, would be consistent with the child's own spanking scenario. When the question of "it" hurting is posed, the child responds affirmatively: the spanking did hurt. But when the interviewer restates the question as *daddy* hurting her, the child says no.

Interviewing a 3-year-old child, then, is an extremely tricky thing to do. Since the child may be the only witness to the suspected sexual abuse, it is necessary to try to ask her questions. The onus is on the interviewer, however, to avoid a schema in which the suspect is assumed to be guilty, particularly in making the interview acceptable evidence for court use. The social worker's therapeutic style of interviewing may be fine for social work, but it falls considerably short of the objectivity required by law. It can cause the interview evidence to be rejected by the court as a type of biased leading question.

The problem of the child's language development is a more difficult obstacle to overcome and there are no easy remedies for the fact that agentive and attributive prepositions may not yet have been learned. Adults are so familiar with prepositions that they assume children, even 3-year-olds, are able to use and understand them in adult ways. This is simply not true, as the above analysis indicates. Rather than asking "Did he touch you *with* his pee-pee?" the interviewer might ask, "Did he put his pee-pee in your butt?" Instead of saying "Show me *with* the dolls," the interviewer might say "Make the dolls do it."

As for the interviewer's inaccurate restatements of what Diana actually said, there is no conceivable justification. She was clearly biased against the accused, Diana's father, and her schema was so strong that it caused her to hear different words from those that Diana actually said.

Despite the presentation of all these problems with the state's interview evidence, the jury found Diana's father guilty. Whether he actually did it or not, the evidence was far too tainted to justify such a conclusion. The emotions of most human beings are very high in child sexual abuse cases, for such offenses are perhaps the most heinous imaginable. It has been said that it is better for ten guilty persons to go free than for one innocent person to be convicted. In child sexual abuse cases, this old adage seems not to apply.

10

On Testifying

Occasionally, in court and out, I am asked whether I consider myself a forensic linguist. The answer I give often surprises the person who asks. I do *not* call myself a forensic linguist. I neither object to the use of the term nor particularly care whether or not I am called one. The fact is, I consider myself a linguist who, in this instance, happens to be carrying out his analysis on data that grows out of a court case. I see no reason to add the word *forensic*, which is a description of the data and the area in which a language problem resides. I do not call myself an educational linguist when I analyze classroom interaction and I did not refer to myself as a medical linguist during the five- or six-year period that I analyzed doctor–patient communication. Besides, I distrust labels, especially new ones. In any case, the word *forensic* conjures up the image of morgues, cadavers, and death. I do not much like the word, regardless of whether or not it may apply to specializations in psychology, sociology, or linguistics.

Over a decade ago, when I first became involved with attorneys in criminal cases, many of my linguist colleagues asked me why I would ever want to do this kind of work. "Why would you want to help a guilty man escape punishment?" was a common question. The issue of guilt or innocence, of course, is not for the linguist to worry about. This is the jury's job alone. I learned very early that one of the worst things an expert witness can do is to get involved with this question. Instead, the linguist analyzes the language evidence from a position of neutrality. In the best and most rational of all possible worlds, the linguist carries out the same analysis whether from the defense or the prosecution's request. If my analysis is only partly favorable to the attorney's case and if the attorney still decides to use my services at trial, he or she runs the risk of hearing the unfavorable analysis during my cross-examination, for the expert witness is always under oath to tell the truth. Even though defense attorneys are under no particular obligation to bring out the dark side of their own case, their witness cannot be so shielded. So, if they sidestep the dark side, there is a better than average chance that alert prosecutors will try to use my analysis against the defendant. If they do, they get it. That's just the way it is.

Most of the criminal cases I have analyzed contain both winnable and losable issues. Although defense attorneys would love to use my testimony for the winnable parts, they often blanch at what I might have to say about the down side of their cases. For this reason, they sometimes use my analysis in ways other then through my testimony. I would estimate, in fact, that I testify in only one out of six cases I work on. Some of those are because of this reason; others are because the client eventually enters a plea bargain or, on rare occasions, when the charges are dismissed before the trial even begins.

The ordeal of testimony is not a pleasant prospect to some people. For one thing, the witness's language rights are seriously reduced in court. The expert must respond only to the questions asked. Sometimes the only possible answer requires a clarification, a qualification, or an explanation but even then the judge may rule that since the question was a yes-or-no type, it must be answered with a *yes* or *no*. This can be a serious problem for an academic, whose world is surrounded with qualification and explanation, a fact which does not go unnoticed by alert prosecutors and defense attorneys alike.

Expert witnesses who submit to examination and cross-examination should expect to be treated in ways quite unfamiliar to what they are used to in an academic setting. For example, they can expect ridicule of various types. They can expect to be submitted to the temptation to get angry. They can expect loaded questions, such as one asked me by Jack Strickland, the prosecutor in *The State of Texas* v. *T. Cullen Davis* in 1980, and referred to in chapter 7:

Strickland: Dr Shuy, when you did this subjective analysis of these tape recordings, what type of tape recorder did you use?
Shuy: I didn't do a subjective analysis.

The expert witness is in a language game and must be alert at all times for traps like Strickland's.

The defense attorney in a criminal case with tape-recorded evidence against his client has a unique problem. The prosecution has available the person, either a law enforcement officer who poses as a criminal or a cooperating witness (people who have already been caught in the investigation and who agree to work with the police to extend the net to additional suspects by agreeing to tape record their conversations with such suspects) to use as courtroom witnesses against the defendant. The tapes are played in court and then these officers or cooperating witnesses take the witness stand and offer their own interpretations of what was going on during these conversations, what they, themselves, intended and what they themselves understood the defendant to be saying.

Defense attorneys have only the defendant to counter such witnesses and, quite frequently, defendants are not very good witnesses on their own behalf. Unlike law enforcement officers, defendants are usually unaccustomed to the courtroom. They often become emotional and inarticulate. They may not provide a convincing performance concerning their own innocence even if they have done nothing wrong. Some defendants are, in fact, quite guilty of some of the charges against them but, in their attempts at self-justification, appear to be guilty of even the unjustified accusations. In such cases, the defense attorney may elect not to let the defendant testify at all, reasoning that it is better to put on no defense than to present one that is unconvincing.

In such cases, the defense attorney needs somebody as a witness on behalf of his client for, as attorney Gerald Goldstein has often said, you cannot cross-examine a tape. That somebody is the linguist who analyzes the conversations in the ways described throughout this book.

In some trials, however, the defense attorney elects to use the testimony of both the defendant and the linguist. In such instances, there may be compelling reasons to put the defendant on the stand. For example, there may be crucial facts to be introduced that only the defendant knows and which only he/she can introduce. In other cases, defendants may be quite articulate and presentable witnesses on their own behalf. In one of the many trials of judges and attorneys in the Chicago Greylord FBI investigation, for example, one defense attorney, Patrick Tuite, asked me to explain my analysis of the wire-tap recordings made surreptitiously in the defendant's, Judge John Laurie's, chambers to the defendant himself. It became clear to me that Judge Laurie was quiet capable of being his own best witness, once he over-came his belief that the government's transcript was correct in many crucial points and once he was calmed down enough to think through his own position. When it was clear that he could do this by himself, the need for my expert witness was lessened. The judge effectively testified on his own behalf and was eventually acquitted.

Some attorneys with whom I work regularly use my analysis only to assist the planning and theory of their cases. In fact, this is exactly how the Department of Justice has used my linguistic services to date. On two different occasions the Public Integrity Section of the US Department of Justice has asked me to review large numbers of tape-recorded conversations that they planned to present as evidence against defendants (one of whom was a prominent Federal judge). I prepared transcripts of these conversations and carried out analyses of their structure. I then met with attorneys from the Justice Department and outlined both the strengths and weaknesses of their case, based on these tapes. As noted earlier, the government did not call me as an expert witness in either case, for various reasons. For one thing, the cases against these defendants were very strong, making my testimony less necessary. Secondly, as one Justice Department attorney, Ralph Martin, advised me, the only reason they would use me as an expert witness was to counter the defense, if they should happen to use a linguist on their side of the case. Upon reviewing possible defense theories, I could see no way that any linguist called by the defense could come up with any analysis that significantly differed from my own. A linguistic analysis is a linguistic analysis. If it happens to fit the defense theory or the prosecution theory or, for that matter, if it actually shapes or contributes to a defense or prosecution theory, it can be usable. The question of whether or not to use it then depends on many other factors, most of which have little or nothing to do with the essence of analysis (such as the apparent perceptiveness of the jurors, the apparent receptivity of the judge, the length of the trial, and many others).

This is not to say that linguists always agree on their analyses of data. They are no different in this respect than scholars in any other discipline. But there is a difference between the type of data that linguists analyze and the type of data used by, for example, psychologists or psychiatrists. As noted earlier, when there are tape recordings of the actual allegedly criminal event, we have primary data (the actual event) to work with, not secondary data (interpretations of the defendant's competence or emotional state based on interviews or tests of the defendant made after the alleged criminal event took place). There is a stability of primary data, the actual event, which is not present in the kinds of testing events used as data by many other fields.

A parallel can be seen in the types of evaluation used by schools. One kind of test is called a performance assessment, the type used by the public officials who issue automobile operators licences. They take the applicant out for a test drive and observe how effectively the driver follows the rules of driving in an actual performance of driving. The contrast with the performance assessment is what is called a discrete point test, the kind of assessment which is far more commonly used by the schools. Such tests are given *after* the teaching has taken place, selecting various small features of learning for individual measurement but ignoring the actual performance in a real life setting. The performance test is located in an actual event; the discrete point test is located in an event intended to represent the actual event but it can in no way be thought of as the actual event itself. The performance test is a measure of primary data; the discrete point test is a measure of the test maker's perception of what represents the actual event and, as such, is secondary data, not primary.

The analysis of primary data is more stable and less subject to interpretation than is the analysis of secondary data. The further one gets from the real event, the more subject the analysis is to variations in interpretation, simply because there are many more interpretations involved in the construction of the measures used in analyzing secondary data. Psychologists and psychiatrists used as expert witnesses, for example, often do not have the luxury of primary data. Their analysis is of the defendant (or some other participant) apart from the alleged criminal event itself. Their tools are professionally accepted tests, measures and categorizations, but not ones that analyze the actual event in question.

This is not to demean the value of psychology or psychiatry in the disposition of a criminal case, for the contributions of these fields can be very helpful. I make this comparison only to show the difference between such analysis and linguistic analysis. Nor do I want to imply that there is anything wrong with interpretations and opinions, for the major goal of an expert is to provide such interpretations and opinions. Indeed, all sciences have rigorous methods of gathering and analyzing data, all of which lead to interpretations, generalizations, and applications. But the amount and type of interpretation increases proportionally as the analysis is distanced from the actual event. Linguists analyze the actual event (or as much of it as is revealed by a real time recording of it) while other fields analyze the participants or artifact objects (such as bullets, skid marks, weapons) long after the actual event is over. Furthermore, at least in cases where the events are language crimes as described in this book, the linguist has analytical tools to discover the clues to participants' intentions and state of mind *during* the actual event, not afterward.

There has been no definitive history of the use of linguistics in the American courts. Linguists do not keep a central file of such activities and, short of informal discussions, there is no easy way to answer such questions as "How many linguists have testified in criminal cases?" Yet this question keeps popping up in cross-examination and keeps being answered with vagueness. I know of only six American linguists who have actually been admitted as expert witnesses in criminal trials. There may be more, I just don't know. This figure does not include phoneticians who have testified on matters of voice identification at trial. Nor does it include linguists who have served as expert witnesses in civil trials (on cases involving trademarks, product liability, insurance disputes, slander, libel, contract disputes and others), where the list is much longer.

In the future, however, one can expect much more extensive use of linguists in court proceedings. A few prominent cases and a few effective experiences with linguists will lead more and more attorneys to call on our services.

Index

Lightning Source UK Ltd.
Milton Keynes UK
UKOW030403190912

199210UK00001B/229/A